英語で読む大統領演説

宮本陽一郎

英語で読む大統領演説 （'20）

©2020　宮本陽一郎

装丁・ブックデザイン：畑中　猛

s-64

まえがき

　この授業を履修するみなさんの多くは，20世紀という時代を生きた経験をお持ちと思います。20世紀がどんな時代だったか，その歴史を振り返るとき，そこに必ず「アメリカ」という存在が影を落とすことは，ひとつの大きな特徴でしょう。ケネディ大統領の暗殺事件が幼い頃の記憶として残っている，あるいは学生時代にヴェトナム反戦運動を経験した，ハリウッド映画やロックに憧れて青春時代を過ごした，アメリカの豊かな生活に憧れて育った——人によってその記憶はさまざまだと思います。しかし「アメリカ」抜きに20世紀の記憶を語ることは困難です。そのような時代のなかで英語は準国際公用語としての位置を占めるようになり，それゆえに私たちは英語を習得したり，苦手意識を持ったりしたことになります。

　この授業では，英語だけを学ぶのではなく，英語とアメリカがこのような存在感を良きにつけ悪しきにつけ持つようになった時代そのものについて考えることを，テーマとしていきたいと思います。取り上げるアメリカ大統領の演説は，「アメリカ」をめぐる歴史の，最もドラマティックな瞬間に発せられた言葉の記録です。歴代の大統領が，歴史的な瞬間のなかで，それぞれに「アメリカ」を語り演じます。授業を履修するみなさんは，自分の英語力について得意か苦手かという自意識をいったん保留して，私たちにとっての「アメリカ」とはなんだったのか考えてみてください。その思考の過程のなかで，知らず識らずに英語を使っていたというのが，この授業の理想的なかたちです。

　私たちが自転車に乗れるようになったり，泳げるようになったりする
とき，何が起こるのでしょうか？単純な練習の積み重ねだけではなく，
何かのきっかけがあって，〈自転車に乗れる〉あるいは〈泳げる〉とい
う心理が作り出されるのでしょう。この授業で取り上げる言葉のドラマ
を体感することが，そのようなきっかけになることを，願っています。

　さらに放送授業では，シオドア・ローズヴェルトゆかりのアメリカ自
然史博物館，フランクリン・D・ローズヴェルト記念図書館・博物館，
オクラホマシティー・ナショナル・メモリアル，ロナルド・レーガン記
念図書館・博物館を訪ね，それぞれの演説にゆかりの記念碑や展示を見
るとともに，館員の方々の解説を聞く機会も設けます。みなさんもいっ
しょにそこを訪れた気分で，館員の方々のガイドに耳を傾けてくださ
い。あまり自分のリスニング能力など気にせずに，ああそうかと，たと
えば目の前にあるモニュメントの意味が理解できたとしたら，これも大
切なきっかけになります。

　履修者のみなさんが目指す語学力は，さまざまだと思います。英語の
資格試験を目指す人もいれば，仕事や研究で英語を使いこなせるように
なりたいという人，あるいは高度な教養として英語力を身につけたいと
いう人もいるでしょう。どのような目標にも使えるようにこの授業を設
計したつもりです。それぞれの必要に応じて，各チャプターに用意され
た課題に取り組んでください。放送大学在校生のみなさんは，学内専用
のシステム WAKABA にアップロードした学習教材も活用して，発展
学習にもチャレンジすることができます。

　このように歴史的な映像と海外ロケ映像をフル活用した英語の授業

は，一般の大学の英語の授業のなかでは望みえません。長年の夢だった授業を作る機会が与えられたことを，たいへんありがたく感じています。不抜の忍耐力で印刷教材の作成を見守ってくださった編集者の伊藤博さん，放送授業の製作について主任講師の無茶振りに臨機応変に対応してくださったディレクターの岩崎真さん，すべてにわたり万全の統括をしてくださったプロデューサーの草川康之さん，そしてスタジオ収録と海外ロケの収録に携わってくださったすべてのスタッフのみなさん，印刷教材の査読の労をとってくださった先生方——たくさんのみなさんのお力を借りて，この授業は完成しました。この場を借りて心より御礼を申し上げたいと思います。

2019 年 10 月
宮本陽一郎

6

目次

まえがき　　　3

Chapter 1 ｜ Introduction　　9
　1. アメリカの世紀　10
　2. 英語は得意ですか、苦手ですか？　11
　3. 訳すことと、わかること　13
　4. ヴォキャブラリー　15
　5. 全体から部分へ　18

Chapter 2 ｜ Paragraph Reading　　21
　1. アメリカの世紀と英語　22
　2. Five-Paragraph Essay　23
　3. パラグラフ　24
　4. アウトライン　26
　5. 演説：論証のドラマ　28

Chapter 3 ｜ Theodore Roosevelt's　37
"The Strenuous Life"
Speech (1899)

Chapter 4 ｜ Franklin D.　49
Roosevelt's First
Inaugural Address
(1933)

Chapter 5 | Franklin D. Roosevelt's First Fireside Chat (1933) | 59

Chapter 6 | Eleanor Roosevelt's Speech on Human Rights (1951) | 69

Chapter 7 | Harry Truman's "Truman Doctrine" Speech (1947) | 75

Chapter 8 | John F. Kennedy's Cuban Missile Crisis Speech (1962) | 83

Chapter 9 | John F. Kennedy's American University Commencement Address (1963) | 93

Chapter 10 | Lyndon B. Johnson's "The Great Society" Speech (1964) | 103

8

Chapter 11 | Jimmy Carter's 113
"Crisis of Confidence"
Speech (1979)

Chapter 12 | Ronald Reagan's 127
"Space Shuttle
Challenger Disaster"
Speech (1986)

Chapter 13 | Ronald Regan's 135
Alzheimer's Letter
(1994)

Chapter 14 | Bill Clinton's 141
Oklahoma Bombing
Memorial Prayer
Service Address
(1995)

Chapter 15 | Barack Obama's 151
"A More Perfect
Union" Speech (2008)

問題解答　162

Chapter 1 | Introduction

(Photo by Getty Images)

　授業を始めるにあたり，この授業でなぜアメリカ合衆国の 20 世紀の大統領の演説を取り上げるかを解説する。そして英語が「わかる」というのがどのようなことを指すのか，英語の授業を通じてどのようなスキルを身につけるのかを考える。

1. アメリカの世紀

この授業では，20世紀のアメリカ合衆国の大統領たちの演説を，教材として取り上げます。

1947年2月17日号の『ライフ』誌に，発行人であるヘンリー・ルースが「アメリカの世紀（The American Century）」と題する社説を掲載し，20世紀は「アメリカの世紀（The American Century）」つまりアメリカ合衆国が世界のリーダーになる時代となるだろうという主張を展開しました。それがよいことなのか悪いことなのか，さまざまな見方があると思いますが，しかし地上にある200近い国家のなかで，アメリカ合衆国が突出した存在感をもった時代が，前世紀にあったことは確かでしょう。

この授業で読み聞きそして見るのは，アメリカ合衆国が世界のなかで例外的な役割を担っている，あるいは担わなければいけないという夢を，その最前線で大統領として生きた人たちの生々しい言葉であり，そしてドラマです。

それを理想主義として讃えるか，自己陶酔として批判するか，その判断を下すのは少し待って，言葉の世界を探索してみることにしましょう。国民の4分の1が失業し飢えて絶望しているという状況のなかで，就任式の壇上にあがった1933年のフランクリン・D・ローズヴェルト大統領は，国民にいったいどんな言葉を投げかけるでしょう。アメリカ本土のわずか90マイル沖にあるキューバに，ソビエトの核ミサイルが配備されつつあることを知り，核戦争の危機に立たされてしまったジョン・F・ケネディ大統領は，全米放送のテレビカメラに向かい，国民にいったいどんな言葉を発するでしょう。すべての言葉にはドラマがあります。

　また20世紀最初の大統領であるシオドア・ローズヴェルトから，バラク・オバマ前大統領に至る大統領たちの言葉をたどっていくことは，単にアメリカ合衆国の歴史を理解するというだけではなく，20世紀を生きた人たちの歴史を見直す，一つの切り口になるであろうと思います。

　こうした問題に関心を持っていただくことは，この科目の英語の授業としてのねらいとも関わります。一定のレベルの語学力，例えば日本の高等学校卒業レベルの英語力を身につけた人が，そのもうひとつ上のレベルの語学力を身につけるために必要なのは，英語を学ぶという意識から，英語を使って学ぶという意識──つまり，英語を使って感じたり，理解したり，思考したり，表現したりするという意識への転換です。

　この授業では，記録映像とロケ映像をふんだんに使って，それぞれの演説のドラマを再現し，履修者のみなさんにはそこに飛び込んで，感じ考えていただきたいと思います。そのなかで英語を学ぶというよりは，英語が自然に自分の思考の一部になっていたという体験が大切です。

2.　英語は得意ですか，苦手ですか？

　英語の授業を担当するとき，最初の授業の際に，履修者たちに，英語が得意か苦手か，もし苦手であるとすればなぜかを聞いてみることがあります。返ってくる答えはいつもほぼ同じで，苦手だという人が圧倒的に多く，苦手である理由はヴォキャブラリーの不足と答える人が圧倒的に多く，文法知識の不足を訴える人の数がそれに続きます。

　これはあまりにも当然です。英語の文章を読もうとして，そこに知らない言葉があれば，とくに知らない言葉がたくさんあれば，「わからない」という反応が起こるのは当然です。しかしここにはいくつかの重要な誤解があります。

　例えば，歌詞が英語である音楽を聞くとき，すべての歌詞が聞き取れなくても，目の前に歌詞の対訳がなくても，その歌がわかります。歌詞の対訳カードから目を離さずに聞けば，その歌がよりよくわかるということにはならないでしょう。むしろ音楽に感動する妨げにすらなるかも知れません。

　この授業で取り上げる演説というジャンルは，歌曲とそれほど遠くかけ離れてはいません。声の抑揚やめりはり，さらには身振りや表情も，コミュニケーションの不可欠の部分をなします。そうした要素をすべてシャットアウトしてしまえば，たしかに英語による演説はわかりにくいということになるでしょうし，自分のヴォキャブラリーの不足ばかりを感じることになるでしょう。しかし，そのように感じる必要はまったくありません。

　例えばマーティン・ルーサー・キング・ジュニア牧師の有名な "I have a dream" 演説はどこかで見て聞いた経験があると思いますが，たとえそこに 30% 知らない単語が入っていても，50% の単語が正確に聞き取れなかったとしても，メッセージはしっかりと心に届くはずです。この演説のクライマックスで，キング牧師は "I have a dream that ..." で始まるセンテンスを 5 回，"Let freedom ring" を 10 回繰り返しています。そのすべてを例えば日本語に訳すことができなくても，その修辞目的——つまり何を言おうとしているか，何を強調しようとしているか——は前後関係や声のトーンから十分に感じ取れるはずです。雄弁術とはそのようなものです。

　これは演説だけの，特別な事情ではありません。ごく日常的な会話であっても，そこにはリズムも音程も強弱もあります。それもコミュニケーションの道具のうちです。そうした要素をシャットアウトして，単語とその発音そして文法だけに頼ってコミュニケーションをとろうとす

れば，英語で話すことも聞くことも非常に難しくなるでしょう。そこから話すこと聞くことへの苦手意識が生まれるのは当然です。

　歌曲でも，演説でも，日常会話でもない，例えば論説文を読む場合はどうでしょうか？そこにも私たち非母語話者の理解を助けてくれる要素があります。それは論理です。センテンスには構文があるのと同様に，文全体には論理があります。具体的に言えば次のチャプターで解説するパラグラフの構造です。ひとつひとつの単語の意味だけからセンテンスの意味を理解するのはたいへんな作業になると思いますが，＜主語＋動詞＞あるいは＜主語＋動詞＋目的語＞という構造が身についていれば，センテンスの意味ははるかに理解しやすくなります。同様に，英語で書かれた文章は，パラグラフ構造が非常に明解です。パラグラフという構造が身についていれば，理解は大いに助けられます。論理の力を無視して，あくまでヴォキャブラリーと文法知識だけに頼って，英語の論説文を読もうとすれば，「わからない」と感じられて当然です。

　そもそも英語が「わかる」というのは，どういうことなのでしょうか。たとえすべての単語の下にシャープペンシルで単語の意味を書き込んでも，たとえノートに全訳を作ったとしても，それは英文を理解したということにはなりません。例えばこの授業で取り上げる大統領演説を読んでそれがわかったというのは，その演説について賛成であれ反対であれ，何か聞き手／読み手としての意見が生まれれば，それは「わかった」ことの証です。同様に論説文を読んだときに，その内容についての思考が始まれば，それは「わかった」ことの証です。

3.　訳すことと，わかること

　訳すこと，つまり英語を日本語に変換すること，あるいは日本語を英

語に変換することだけをゴールと錯覚してしまうと，英語を使って思考する，英語を使って仕事をする，英語を使ってコミュニケートするというレベルには，なかなか到達できません。

　この授業では，各チャプターの本文の後に，「I」として3〜4問の設問が設けてあります。この3つか4つの問いに答えられたら，演説全体の要点は「わかった」ということになります。つまりその演説の内容について，自分なりに考えたり議論したりすることはできるはずです。英文をすべて日本語に置き換えることをゴールとせず，この3つから4つのポイントをクリアしたら，そこが当面のゴールだと意識を転換してみてください。それぞれの問いは，内容理解をチェックする試験というよりは，演説全体を理解するためのヒントあるいは道案内と考えてください。

　また，「I」のそれぞれの問いのなかで，「日本語に訳しなさい」という指示は，1回も使っていないことに注目してください。その代わりに，必要な情報が書いてあるセンテンスを全体のなかから「抜き出しなさい」，そして「その意味するところをできるだけ簡潔な日本語で説明しなさい」という設問になっています。センテンスを抜き出す作業は，演説全体のなかでいちばん大切なことが書いてある3〜4箇所にいわばアンダーラインを引く作業です。アンダーラインを引いた箇所をすべて日本語に訳す必要はありません。むしろそれをできるだけ簡潔に頭のなかにまとめることが大切です。

　設問の「II」は，すべてのチャプターで「次の一節について，最善の日本語訳を作成してみてください」という指示に統一してあります。選んだ箇所は，演説全体のなかでいちばん大事な箇所，しばしば引用される箇所です。これについては，ただ日本語に訳すのではなく，最善の日本語訳，最善の翻訳を作ってみてください。ここでは，すべての単語の

辞書的な意味を理解し，そして文法構造を理解したうえで，それぞれの文のトーンやニュアンスまで伝わるような名訳を，少し時間をかけて作ってみてください。「訳す」という意識はしばしば理解の妨げになりますが，「翻訳する」という作業は深いレベルでの理解を日本語で表現するという，たいへんクリエイティヴな作業で，私たちの日本語の表現力を最大限に駆使することにもなるでしょう。巻末の問題解答には，私なりの日本語訳を載せておきましたが，それよりもさらによい翻訳を目指してください。

　設問の「I」と「II」に答えたら，その演説は理解できた——つまり必要なポイントはすべて抑えたことになります。

　そして「発展的課題」に進むことができます。ここでは演説全体を理解したうえで，それについて考え始めるための方向が示唆されています。放送授業のなかでは，ここに掲げたいくつかの問いを頭に置いて，演説の解題を試みます。

4.　ヴォキャブラリー

　以上から，英語が苦手であると感じる理由は，ヴォキャブラリーと文法知識の不足だけに由来するのではないこと，また逆にヴァキャブラリーと文法知識があれば英語が理解できるはずだと考えることの問題点を，ご理解いただけたと思います。

　しかし，ヴォキャブラリー力は必要ないということにはなりません。

　ヴォキャブラリー力の養成を図るのが設問「III」です。ここでの指示もすべての章で「辞書を読み，次の5つの単語がどのような意味をとりうるかを理解しましょう」という指示に統一してあります。辞書を引くのではなく読んでください。ここで読む辞書は，例文が豊富な中辞典

以上の辞書，できれば英英辞典を使ってください。私が常用しているのは *American Heritage Dictionary* という最も平均的な辞書で，インターネット上でオンライン検索することも可能です（https://www.ahdictionary.com）。

　ヴォキャブラリー力は必ずしも知っている単語の総数で測られるものではありません。核となる800語程度が十分に使いこなせていることが，より重要です。そのような重要な単語は，例えば「dictionary＝辞書」のよう1対1対応で覚えることはできません。例えばチャプター3で覚える5つの単語のなかの1つは，"dare" です。強いて訳語を1つあてれば，「敢えて…する」というあたりになるでしょうが，それでは本文中に出てきた "Far better it is to dare mighty things, to win glorious triumphs." という文は理解できません。*American Heritage Dictionary* は，"dare" の他動詞としての意味として，以下の3つを挙げ，それぞれの例文を示しています。

1. To have the required for
2. To challenge (someone) to do something requiring boldness
3. To confront boldly; brave

"Far better it is to dare mighty things" という文では，"dare" は3番目の "To confront boldly" の意味で使われており，「壮大な課題に挑戦することのほうがはるかに素晴らしい」という意味になります。「dare＝挑戦」と覚えただけでは，"She dared to criticize her teacher." つまり「彼女は敢えて教師を批判した」あるいは「彼女は勇気をもって教師を批判した」という文は理解できません。

　最も重要な単語は，英語と日本語の1対1対応で丸暗記することはで

きません。そのような単語については，辞書を引くのではなく例文まで含めて読み，そして「どのような意味をとりうるか」を理解することが大切です。

この授業を通じてヴォキャブラリー力をつけたい人は，どうか辞書を引かずに辞書を読んでください。

ヴォキャブラリー力についてもう一点つけくわえたいと思います。

ヴォキャブラリー力は，必ずしも知っている単語の数だけで測られるわけではありません。知らない単語の意味を類推する力もこれに含まれます。例えば "Far better it is to dare mighty things, to win glorious triumphs." について言えば，"to dare mighty things" と "to win glorious triumphs" は同格のコンマで結ばれています。つまり "to dare mighty things" と "to win glorious triumphs" はほぼ同義だということになります。仮に "to dare mighty things" がそれ自体として理解できなくても，"to win glorious triumphs" が理解できれば，その意味は類推可能になります。

非母語話者の英語力を測る国際試験として最も高い信頼性を持つのはTOEFL という試験です。TOEFL のリーディングに関する出題のうち30% 程度は，単語の意味を前後関係から類推させる問題になっており，例えば "'From the scratch' in paragraph 1 is closest in meaning to ..." という設問があり，4 つの選択肢から正解を選ぶという形式になります。言い換えるならこの最も信頼度の高い語学試験を設計した人たちは，リーディングの力の30% は，知らない言葉の意味を前後関係から類推する力にあると考えたことになります。知らない単語を見たら機械的に辞書を引く，あるいは知らない単語には脚注がついていて当然という態度が身についてしまうと，いちばん大切なヴォキャブラリー力が養われなくなってしまいます。

この印刷教材には語釈は1箇所もついていません。

5. 全体から部分へ

TOEFL と日本の大学入試を比較すると，いくつかの違いに気づきます。

日本の大学入試の英語では，高校までの学習範囲から外れた難しい言葉には，語釈をつけることが一般的です。いっぽう TOEFL の場合，難しい言葉や専門用語が出てきてもいっさい語釈はつきません。その理由はすでにおわかりいただけていると思いますが，TOEFL の出題者たちは，そうした語彙の意味を類推する力を重視するからです。

もう1つ，あまり意識されない，しかし重要な違いがあります。

日本の大学入試問題では，本文の後に「下線部(1)を日本語で説明しなさい」「空欄(a)に入る単語を次のなかから選びなさい」「下線部(3)の"this" が指す内容を説明しなさい」といった部分理解に関する設問が続き，最後に全体の論旨についての設問，例えば「本文の内容に合致するものを次のなかから2つ選びなさい」といった設問が来るのが一般的です。

TOEFL ではそれが逆になります。本文の後に最初に来る典型的な質問は，"What is the main topic of this passage?" つまり本文は全体として何について論じていますかという設問です。日本の大学入試とは設問の順序が真逆になっています。

つまり日本の大学入試の英語は，まず単語が理解できて，センテンスが理解できて，文が理解できて，その積み上げによって全体が理解できるという，（一見）自然なモデルに基づいています。

それに対して，TOEFL の英語は，まず全体が理解できて，それに照らして必要に応じて部分を理解して，知らない単語に出会ったらその意

味を論旨や文脈に沿って類推するというモデルに基づいています。

　なぜそんなことが可能なのでしょうか？次のチャプターに進んでください。

Chapter 2 | Paragraph Reading

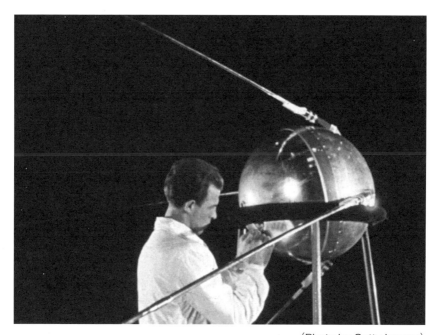

(Photo by Getty Images)

　1957年，ソビエト連邦（当時）は人類初の人工衛星スプートニック1号の打ち上げに成功する。科学技術開発の最先端でソ連の後塵を拝したということは，冷戦期のアメリカにあっては国家存亡の危機としてとらえられた。いわゆるスプートニック危機のなかで，未曾有の規模の教育改革が始まり，それは「作文教育」の抜本的な改革にまで及ぶ。

　最初のTOEFLが実施されたのは，その7年後の1964年のことだった。

1. アメリカの世紀と英語

　今日，英語が世界中で 10 億人以上が用いる準公用語となってしまったのは，必ずしもアメリカ合衆国が，突出した経済大国・軍事大国になってしまったからだけではありません。1957 年のスプートニック危機に始まる大規模な教育改革のなかで，科学技術研究の高度化が図られただけでなく，国語教育つまり英語の読み書きの教え方までもが見直されます。1958 年に制定された国防教育法（National Defense Education Act）に基づく教育改革には，近代語学会（MLA），アメリカ学会（ALA），大学英語協会（CEA）など国語教育に関わる学術団体も協力します。そのなかで学術英語（academic English）という，学術的な情報交換に最適化したスタイルが確立されたことは，英語が準公用語となったことの大きな要因の 1 つです。

　スプートニックの 2 年後の 1959 年には，ウィリアム・ストランク・ジュニアが 1918 年に執筆し，当時は顧みられることもなかった *The Elements of Style* という簡便な文章読本が改訂出版され，ベストセラーになります。*The Elements of Style* は，現在に至るまで，大学生・研究者の必携書として，世界中で読まれています。この文章読本が強調したポイントの 1 つは，センテンスではなくパラグラフに重点をおいた文章の書き方でした。

　これと相前後して，アメリカの大学では大学初年次生のための論文執筆法の授業「フレッシュマン・ライティング・セミナー」が整備され，ここでもパラグラフ主体の論文執筆法の教育が徹底されます。

　1964 年に初めて実施された TOEFL は，その延長線上にあります。

TOEFL のリーディングに出題されるのは，さまざまな分野の教科書の抜粋のみで，それ以外のタイプの文章は出題されません。そしてこうした文章すべてにおいてパラグラフ・ライティングが徹底されているので，まず全体の論旨が最初に読み取れるように構成されています。それゆえに前のチャプターで触れたように，最初の設問は "What is the main topic of this passage?" なのです。

2.　Five-Paragraph Essay

こうした改革のなかで生まれた典型的な作文教育法が "Five-Paragraph Essay" です。小中学校教育の段階で，1 つの論点を 5 つのパラグラフで展開する作文の書き方が徹底的に練習されます。

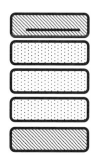

なぜ 5 パラグラフなのか？それは 1 つの論点あるいは主張について，その根拠を 3 つ示すことによって読者を説得するためです。英語の日常会話のなかでも，「根拠はなんだい？」というときに，"Name three examples." という言い方がされます。序論 (Introduction) のパラグラフに続く，本論 (Body) の 3 つのパラグラフが全体の主張を裏づける役割を果たします。そして最後の第 5 パラグラフは結論 (Conclusion) の役割を果たします。

30 ～ 31 ページの文章は，Five-Paragraph Essay のサンプルとして使い回されている文章です。全体の主張 (main thesis) の置かれる場所も決まっていて，原則として第 1 パラグラフの最終センテンスです。したがってこの文章全体の主張は一目瞭然で，"Despite what dog lovers

may believe, cats make excellent housepets." つまり「ネコはよいペットだ」というちょっと子どもっぽい主張です。ここには起承転結の「転」も，序破急の「破」も，サプライズもありません。この主張は最後まで一貫します。

　ただし，「誰がなんと言おうとネコはかわいい」と一方的に主張するだけでは，読者を説得することはできません。書き手はイヌ好き（dog lover）を読み手として想定し，イヌ好きでも納得するような根拠を，1つと言わず3つ示さなければなりません。パラグラフ・ライティングは説得術です。

3.　パラグラフ

（1）1＝1

　パラグラフとは，なんでしょうか？日本語の段落とはまったく違う機能と構造を持ちます。まず第一の特徴は，1 paragraph＝1 topic です。つまり1つのパラグラフの論点は必ず1つ。2つ以上のことを1つのパ

ラグラフで決して述べてはならないというルールです。そしてそれを明確に述べたセンテンスがなければパラグラフは成立しません。このセンテンスをトピック・センテンスと呼びます。センテンスに主語の定位置があり，文章全体に main thesis の定位置があるのと同じように，トピック・センテンスにも定位置があります。それはパラグラフの第1センテンスです。

　30〜31ページの文章のネコ好きの書き手の場合は，この原則どおり

に，第2〜4パラグラフの第1センテンスに，トピック・センテンスを置いています。このセンテンスの意味さえわかれば，少なくともこのパラグラフのトピック（何を言おうとしているか）は，わかるようになっています。別の言い方をすれば，トピック・センテンスを読んだだけで何を言おうとしているかがわからないようなパラグラフは決して書くな──という作文教育がなされます。

　これは美しい文章を書くための方法にはならないかもしれませんが，しかし非母語話者を含むたくさんの人々が，学術的なコミュニケーションをするためにはたいへん便利なルールになります。つまりトピック・センテンス以外のセンテンスが十分に理解できなくても，論をたどっていくことには支障が生じません。逆に書く場合について言うなら，トピック・センテンスさえ明瞭に書けていれば，読者を導いていくことが可能になります。非母語話者にもフレンドリーなコミュニケーション・ルールです。

（2）1＝1＋3

　それぞれのパラグラフの構成についても＜根拠は3つ＞というルールが適用されます。文章全体について，第1パラグラフで提示した main thesis は，それに続く3つのパラグラフでサポートされます。同様に各パラグラフのトピック・センテンスも具体例を挙げるなどして，それに続くセンテンスでサポートしなければなりません。

　30〜31ページのネコ好きの書き手の場合，第2パラグラフの "In the first place, people enjoy the companionship of cats." つまり「ネコといると楽しい」という論点を，3つの具体例を挙げることによりサポート

し，イヌ好きを含む読者たちを説得していきます。説得の方法は，必ずしも具体例 3 つを挙げることだけではありません。因果関係を 3 段階程度でたどったり，あるいは右の図のように比較対照することにより，読者を説得するというかたちも取りえます。

これもまた，非母語話者にたいへんフレンドリーな書法です。例えば第 2 パラグラフの最後に出てくる "Cats will even fetch!" というセンテンスの意味が仮にわからなかったとしても，このパラグラフの修辞目的 (rhetorical purpose) はわかります。つまりこのセンテンスの役割は，「ネコといると楽しい」という論点を裏づけるための 3 つ目の根拠ということになります。同様に第 3 パラグラフの最後に出てくる "declawed" という単語の意味がわからなくても，この部分の修辞目的が，「ネコはおとなしくていい」というこのパラグラフの論点を裏づけることにあるのは理解できます。修辞目的で大くくりに理解することができれば，かりに部分的に理解できない語句があっても，文章全体の意味するところは把握することができます。

30〜31 ページの原文に，パラグラフの構造がわかりやすいようにマークを入れると，32〜33 ページのようになります。

4. アウトライン

1958 年に再版された文章読本 *The Elements of Style* が推奨する文章作法の 1 つは，まずアウトラインを作ってから書くということです。1918 年に最初に刊行されたときにはまったく反響のなかったこの本が，

再版されて今日では世界的なベストセラーになったのは，20世紀のあいだに，アメリカ合衆国が少なからぬ役割を果たしながら，文章の書き方がいかに大きく変化したかを物語っています。アウトラインから書くという書き方がどれほど普及したか——それは，今日世界中で用いられている WORD や PAGES のようなワープロ・ソフトに必ずアウトライナー機能がついていることからも伺えます。まずアウトラインを書き，それからそこに上書きするようにして文章を書いていくというプロセスが自動化されています。

　ネコ好きの著者の場合，＜ネコはいいペットだと思う＞という素朴な想いを，＜イヌは人間の最良の友＞というアンチテーゼ（反対命題）に対置したところから論が始まります。そして著者は，イヌ好きを納得させるための3つの論点を考えます。この段階で，非常に簡略な以下のようなアウトラインが書けたはずです。

ネコはよいペットだ

I.　　ネコといると楽しい

II.　　ネコは行儀がいい

III.　　ネコは手がかからない

　書き始めるためには，I. II. III. それぞれの下に3つ程度の項目を書き込んだ二階層のアウトラインにしなければなりません。たぶん34ページの問1のようなアウトラインになったはずです。原文に照らして空欄をなるべく簡潔に埋めてください。このようにアウトラインを含めれば，この文章はわかったことになります。35ページの問2は，内容把握の

問題です。完成させたアウトラインだけを使って解答できるはずです。

　以上のようなパラグラフ・ライティングの構造を理解するなら，学術英語というスタイルで書かれた文章は，部分理解の積み上げによって全体が理解できるのではなく，まず全体が理解できて，しかるのちに部分が，そしてさらに細部が理解できるというプロセスをとります。つまり＜全体から部分へ＞という読み方になります。日本の大学入試の英語の出題は，これと真逆の＜部分から全体へ＞というシナリオに基づいています。

　どちらが正しいという問題ではありません。文化的な差異です。

5.　演説：論証のドラマ

　これ以降のチャプターで取り上げる演説は，このようなあからさまなパラグラフ構造はとっていません。

　しかしまったく別のタイプの文章を読むということではありません。演説はむしろパラグラフ・ライティングの原点です。まず論点を高らかに提示し，それを例証・論証するプロセスで，読み手・聞き手を説得していくという構造は，演説のなかでは一層ドラマティックに展開します。

　例えばチャプター4で取り上げるフランクリン・D・ローズヴェルトの有名な就任演説の場合，"So, first of all, let me assert my firm belief that the only thing we have to fear is fear itself." という一見意味不明の主張が高らかに告げられ，一瞬の間を置いてからトーンを変えて，なぜそう言えるのかが，3つのポイントで示されていきます。そのようにして聴衆を説得していくプロセスが，この演説の雄弁さであり弁証法的

なドラマでもあります。

　このチャプターで紹介した，パラグラフ・ライティングは無味乾燥に思えるかもしれません。練習問題として掲げた文章は，どのような尺度で考えても美文とは言えません。しかしそのルーツは政治演説に見られる雄弁術であり，非常に人間的なドラマでもあります。

"A dog is man's best friend." That common saying may contain some truth, but dogs are not the only animal friend whose companionship people enjoy. For many people, a cat is their best friend. Despite what dog lovers may believe, cats make excellent housepets.

In the first place, people enjoy the companionship of cats. Many cats are affectionate. They will snuggle up and ask to be petted, or scratched under the chin. Who can resist a purring cat? If they're not feeling affectionate, cats are generally quite playful. They love to chase balls and feathers, or just about anything dangling from a string. They especially enjoy playing when their owners are participating in the game. Contrary to popular opinion, cats can be trained. Using rewards and punishments, just like with a dog, a cat can be trained to avoid unwanted behavior or perform tricks. Cats will even fetch!

In the second place, cats are civilized members of the household. Unlike dogs, cats do not bark or make other loud noises. Most cats don't even meow very often. They generally lead a quiet existence. Cats also don't often have "accidents." Mother cats train their kittens to use the litter box, and most cats will use it without fail from that time on. Even stray cats usually understand the concept when shown the box and will use it regularly. Cats do have claws, and owners must make provision for this. A tall scratching post in a favorite cat area of the house will often keep the cat content to leave the furniture alone. As a last resort, of course, cats can be declawed.

Lastly, one of the most attractive features of cats as housepets is their ease of care. Cats do not have to be walked. They get plenty of exercise in the house as they play, and they do their business in the litter box. Cleaning a litter box is a quick, painless procedure. Cats also take care of their own grooming. Bathing a cat is almost never necessary because under ordinary circumstances cats clean themselves. Cats are more particular about personal cleanliness than people are. In addition, cats can be left home alone for a few hours without fear. Unlike some pets, most cats will not destroy the furnishings when left alone. They are content to go about their usual activities until their owners return.

Cats are low maintenance, civilized companions. People who have small living quarters or less time for pet care should appreciate these characteristics of cats. However, many people who have plenty of space and time still opt to have a cat because they love the cat personality. In many ways, cats are the ideal housepet.

(©Kathy Livingston)

"A dog is man's best friend." That common saying may contain some truth, but dogs are not the only animal friend whose companionship people enjoy. For many people, a cat is their best friend. **Despite what dog lovers may believe, cats make excellent housepets.**

In the first place, people enjoy the companionship of cats. ❶ Many cats are affectionate. They will snuggle up and ask to be petted, or scratched under the chin. Who can resist a purring cat? ❷ If they're not feeling affectionate, cats are generally quite playful. They love to chase balls and feathers, or just about anything dangling from a string. They especially enjoy playing when their owners are participating in the game. ❸ Contrary to popular opinion, cats can be trained. Using rewards and punishments, just like with a dog, a cat can be trained to avoid unwanted behavior or perform tricks. Cats will even fetch!

In the second place, cats are civilized members of the household. ❶ Unlike dogs, cats do not bark or make other loud noises. Most cats don't even meow very often. They generally lead a quiet existence. ❷ Cats also don't often have "accidents." Mother cats train their kittens to use the litter box, and most cats will use it without fail from that time on. Even stray cats usually understand the concept when shown the box and will use it regularly. ❸ Cats do have claws, and owners must make provision for this. A tall scratching post in a favorite cat area of the house will often keep the cat content to leave the furniture alone. As a last resort, of course, cats can be declawed.

Lastly, one of the most attractive features of cats as housepets is their ease of care. ❶ Cats do not have to be walked. They get plenty of exercise in the house as they play, and they do their business in the litter box. Cleaning a litter box is a quick, painless procedure. ❷ Cats also take care of their own grooming. Bathing a cat is almost never necessary because under ordinary circumstances cats clean themselves. Cats are more particular about personal cleanliness than people are. ❸ In addition, cats can be left home alone for a few hours without fear. Unlike some pets, most cats will not destroy the furnishings when left alone. They are content to go about their usual activities until their owners return.

Cats are low maintenance, civilized companions. People who have small living quarters or less time for pet care should appreciate these characteristics of cats. However, many people who have plenty of space and time still opt to have a cat because they love the cat personality. **In many ways, cats are the ideal housepet.**

34

問 1　空欄に英語を補い，アウトラインを完成させなさい。（なるべく
　　　簡潔に）

I. Thesis: _____.

II. Topic: People enjoy the companionship of cats.
　　　　　A. Cats are _____.
　　　　　B. Cats are playful.
　　　　　C. Cats can be trained.

III. Topic: Cats are _____.
　　　　　D. Cats do not bark.
　　　　　E. Cats don't have _____.
　　　　　F. Cats do have claws. But provisions can be made.

IV. Topic: _____.
　　　　　G. _____.
　　　　　H. _____.
　　　　　I. Cats can be left home alone.

V. Conclusion:
　　　　_____.

問2　下記の問いに日本語で，なるべく簡潔に答えなさい。

1. この文章の主張は何ですか。

　　　　―――――――――――――――――――――――――――.

2. ネコが行儀の良い伴侶（"civilized companion"）であると筆者が主
   張する根拠は何ですか。3つ挙げなさい。

　　　　1　―――――――――――――――――――――――――.
　　　　2　―――――――――――――――――――――――――.
　　　　3　―――――――――――――――――――――――――.

3. ネコが飼いやすいペットであると筆者が主張する根拠は何ですか。
   3つ挙げなさい。

　　　　1　―――――――――――――――――――――――――.
　　　　2　―――――――――――――――――――――――――.
　　　　3　―――――――――――――――――――――――――.

4. ネコは，どのような人のペットとして最適であると筆者は述べてい
   ますか。

　　　　―――――――――――――――――――――――――――.

Chapter 3 | Theodore Roosevelt's "The Strenuous Life" Speech (1899)

（Photo by Getty Images）

シオドア・ローズヴェルト。20 世紀最初のアメリカ大統領。

最初に自動車に乗った大統領，最初に飛行機に乗った大統領，最初に潜水艦に乗った大統領，最初に在任中に海外に出た大統領，当時最年少の大統領。

牧場主，学者，探検家，科学者，自然保護者，博物学者，政治家，歴史家，ヒューマニスト，軍人，愛国者。そしてノーベル平和賞受賞者。

小児喘息に苦しみ，成人するのは困難と思われていた病弱な少年は，からだを鍛え上げ，西部でカウボーイとして生活し，桁外れのアメリカ大統領になった。

1912 年には，暗殺者の銃弾を胸に受けるが，銃弾すらその強靭なからだを貫通することなく，ローズヴェルトはそのまま 90 分近く演説を続けた。

ローズヴェルトは "Strenuous Life" つまり奮闘的な生活，過酷な生活を通じて心身を鍛えることの美徳を説き続けた。

(Photo by Getty Images)

[1] In speaking to you, men of the greatest city of the West, men of the State which gave to the country Lincoln and Grant, men who preeminently and distinctly embody all that is most American in the American character, I wish to preach, not the doctrine of ignoble ease, but the doctrine of the strenuous life, the life of toil and effort, of labor and strife; to preach that highest form of success which comes, not to the man who desires mere easy peace, but to the man who does not shrink from danger, from hardship or from bitter toil, and who out of these wins the splendid ultimate triumph.

[2] A life of slothful ease, a life of that peace which springs merely from lack either of desire or of power to strive after great things, is as little worthy of a nation as of an individual. I ask only that what every self-respecting American demands from himself and from his sons shall be demanded of the American nation as a whole. Who among you would teach your boys that case, that peace, is to be the first Consideration in their eyes — to be the ultimate goal after which they strive? You men of Chicago have made this city great, you men of Illinois have done your share, and more than your share, in making America great, because you neither preach nor practice such a doctrine. You work

yourselves, and you bring up your sons to work. If you are rich and are worth your salt, you will teach your sons that though they may have leisure, it is not to be spent in idleness; for wisely used leisure merely means that those who possess it, being free from the necessity of working for their livelihood, are all the more bound to carry on some kind of non-remunerative work in science, in letters, in art, in exploration, in historical research — work of the type we most need in this country, the successful carrying out of which reflects most honor upon the nation.

[3] We do not admire the man of timid peace. We admire the man who embodies victorious effort; the man who never wrongs his neighbor, who is prompt to help a friend, but who has those virile qualities necessary to win in the stern strife of actual life. It is hard to fail, but it is worse never to have tried to succeed. In this life we get nothing save by effort. Freedom from effort in the present merely means that there has been stored up effort in the past. A man can be freed from the necessity of work only by the fact that he or his fathers before him have worked to good purpose. If the freedom thus purchased is used aright, and the man still does actual work, though of a different kind, whether as a writer or a general, whether in the field of politics or in the field of exploration and adventure, he shows he deserves his good fortune.

[4] But if he treats this period of freedom from the need of actual

labor as a period, not of preparation, but of mere enjoyment, even though perhaps not of vicious enjoyment, he shows that he is simply a cumberer of the earth's surface, and he surely unfits himself to hold his own with his fellows if the need to do so should again arise. A mere life of ease is not in the end a very satisfactory life, and, above all, it is a life which ultimately unfits those who follow it for serious work in the world.

[5] In the last analysis a healthy state can exist only when the men and women who make it up lead clean, vigorous, healthy lives; when the children are so trained that they shall endeavor, not to shirk difficulties, but to overcome them; not to seek ease, but to know how to wrest triumph from toil and risk. The man must be glad to do a man's work, to dare and endure and to labor; to keep himself, and to keep those dependent upon him. The woman must be the housewife, the helpmeet of the homemaker, the wise and fearless mother of many healthy children. In one of Daudet's powerful and melancholy books he speaks of "the fear of maternity, the haunting terror of the young wife of the present day." When such words can be truthfully written of a nation, that nation is rotten to the heart's core. When men fear work or fear righteous war, when women fear motherhood, they tremble on the brink of doom; and well it is that they should vanish from the earth, where they are fit subjects for the scorn of all men and women who are themselves strong and brave and high-minded.

[6] As it is with the individual, so it is with the nation. It is a base untruth to say that happy is the nation that has no history. Thrice happy is the nation that has a glorious history. Far better it is to dare mighty things, to win glorious triumphs, even though checkered by failure, than to take rank with those poor spirits who neither enjoy much nor suffer much, because they live in the gray twilight that knows not victory nor defeat. If in 1861 the men who loved the Union had believed that peace was the end of all things, and war and strife the worst of all things, and had acted up to their belief, we would have saved hundreds of thousands of lives, we would have saved hundreds of millions of dollars. Moreover, besides saving all the blood and treasure we then lavished, we would have prevented the heartbreak of many women, the dissolution of many homes, and we would have spared the country those months of gloom and shame when it seemed as if our armies marched only to defeat. We could have avoided all this suffering simply by shrinking from strife. And if we had thus avoided it, we would have shown that we were weaklings, and that we were unfit to stand among the great nations of the earth. Thank God for the iron in the blood of our fathers, the men who upheld the wisdom of Lincoln, and bore sword or rifle in the armies of Grant! Let us, the children of the men who proved themselves equal to the mighty days, let us, the children of the men who carried the great Civil War to a triumphant conclusion, praise the God of our fathers that the ignoble counsels of peace were rejected; that the suffering and

loss, the blackness of sorrow and despair, were unflinchingly faced, and the years of strife endured; for in the end the slave was freed, the Union restored, and the mighty American republic placed once more as a helmeted queen among nations.

. . .

[7] I preach to you, then, my countrymen, that our country calls not for the life of ease but for the life of strenuous endeavor. The twentieth century looms before us big with the fate of many nations. If we stand idly by, if we seek merely swollen, slothful ease and ignoble peace, if we shrink from the hard contests where men must win at hazard of their lives and at the risk of all they hold dear, then the bolder and stronger peoples will pass us by, and will win for themselves the domination of the world. Let us therefore boldly face the life of strife, resolute to do our duty well and manfully; resolute to uphold righteousness by deed and by word; resolute to be both honest and brave, to serve high ideals, yet to use practical methods. Above all, let us shrink from no strife, moral or physical, within or without the nation, provided we are certain that the strife is justified, for it is only through strife, through hard and dangerous endeavor, that we shall ultimately win the goal of true national greatness.

(Photo by Getty Images)

I. この演説の内容について，以下に答えなさい。

  A. この演説の Thesis，各パラグラフのトピック，そして結論を取り出すと，以下のようなアウトラインになります。これのみに基づいて，演説の内容を簡潔な日本語で要約しなさい。

- **Thesis:** I wish to preach ... the doctrine of the strenuous life.
- **Paragraph 2 :** A life of slothful ease ... is as little worthy of a nation as of an individual.
- **Paragraph 3 :** We do not admire the man of timid peace. We admire the man who embodies victorious effort ... .
- **Paragraph 4 :** But if he treats this period of freedom from the need of actual labor ... , he shows that he is simply a cumberer of the earth's surface.
- **Paragraph 5 :** In the last analysis a healthy state can exist only when the men and women who make it up lead clean, vigorous, healthy lives ... .
- **Paragraph 6 :** Thrice happy is the nation that has a glorious history ... .
- **Conclusion:** Above all, let us shrink from no strife, moral or physical, within or without the nation, provided we are certain that the strife is justified ... .

  B. シオドア・ローズヴェルトはこの演説のなかで，"Strenuous Life" という言葉を，どのような意味で使っていますか。第1パラグラフを読み直し，なるべく簡潔に日本語で説明しなさい。

  C. シオドア・ローズヴェルトは，戦争と平和に関する通念を敢えて

覆し，平和より戦争が大切だという逆説を展開しています。その
理由を最も明瞭に述べているセンテンスを，第6パラグラフから
抜き出し，その意味するところを簡潔に日本語で説明しなさい。

II. 次の一節について，最善の日本語訳を作成してみてください。

And if we had thus avoided it, we would have shown that we
were weaklings, and that we were unfit to stand among the great
nations of the earth. Thank God for the iron in the blood of our
fathers, the men who upheld the wisdom of Lincoln, and bore
sword or rifle in the armies of Grant! Let us, the children of the
men who proved themselves equal to the mighty days, let us, the
children of the men who carried the great Civil War to a
triumphant conclusion, praise the God of our fathers that the
ignoble counsels of peace were rejected; that the suffering and
loss, the blackness of sorrow and despair, were unflinchingly
faced, and the years of strife endured; for in the end the slave
was freed, the Union restored, and the mighty American republic
placed once more as a helmeted queen among nations.

III. 辞書を読み，次の5つの単語がどのような意味をとりうるかを理
解しましょう。

vigorous

In the last analysis a healthy state can exist only when the men and
women who make it up lead clean, **vigorous**, healthy lives.

dare, endure

The man must be glad to do a man's work, to **dare** and **endure** and
to labor; to keep himself, and to keep those dependent upon him.
Far better it is to **dare** mighty things, to win glorious triumphs.
Years of strife **endured**.

risk

They know how to wrest triumph from toil and **risk**.
Men must win at hazard of their lives and at the **risk** of all they
hold dear.

strife

Above all, let us shrink from no **strife**, moral or physical, within or
without the nation, provided we are certain that the **strife** is
justified, for it is only through **strife**, through hard and dangerous
endeavor, that we shall ultimately win the goal of true national
greatness.

発展的課題

A. シオドア・ローズヴェルトは，本文の中で，"great" という言葉を 7 回も使っています。とくに第 2 パラグラフの "making America great" は，トランプ大統領が選挙キャンペーンや就任演説で用いた "making America great again" という表現の原型と考えてもよいでしょう。またチャプター 10 で取り上げるジョンソン大統領の演説のなかで主張されている「偉大な社会（The Great Society)」という理念も，シオドア・ローズヴェルトのこの演説を連想させます。本文のなかで，ローズヴェルトは "great" というともすれば空疎な賛辞に，どのような内実を与えているか，考えてみましょう。

B. ローズヴェルトのジェンダー観（社会の中での男性の役割／女性の役割）について，考えるところを述べなさい。

C. 放送授業のなかでの解説を聞いたうえで，それを参考にしながら，次頁の写真の影像の意味を，1 分間程度の英語で口頭により説明してみましょう。下書きを書いてもかまいませんが，なるべくそれを見ないように話してみてください。

（撮影：宮本陽一郎）

Chapter 4 | Franklin D. Roosevelt's First Inaugural Address (1933)

（Photo by Getty Images）

　1929 年 10 月 24 日，ウォール街の株式が大暴落するとともに大恐慌が始まる。アメリカ人の 4 人に 1 人が失業するという，未曾有の経済的破局がアメリカ中を包み，世界中に広がる。ヨーロッパではナチスが台頭していた。

　大恐慌からの回復の兆しも見えない 1933 年 3 月 4 日，第 32 代大統領フランクリン・D・ローズヴェルトが就任式の壇上に立つ。

　フランクリン・D・ローズヴェルトは，合衆国史上ただ 1 人，3 期にわたり大統領をつとめ，ローズヴェルトのもとでアメリカは，大恐慌を克服し，第二次世界大戦を戦う。

[1] I am certain that my fellow Americans expect that on my induction into the Presidency I will address them with a candor and a decision which the present situation of our Nation impels. This is preeminently the time to speak the truth, the whole truth, frankly and boldly. Nor need we shrink from honestly facing conditions in our country today. This great

(Photo by Getty Images)

Nation will endure as it has endured, will revive and will prosper. So, first of all, let me assert my firm belief that the only thing we have to fear is fear itself — nameless, unreasoning, unjustified terror which paralyzes needed efforts to convert retreat into advance. In every dark hour of our national life a leadership of frankness and vigor has met with that understanding and support of the people themselves which is essential to victory. I am convinced that you will again give that support to leadership in these critical days.

[2] In such a spirit on my part and on yours we face our common difficulties. They concern, thank God, only material things. Values have shrunken to fantastic levels; taxes have risen; our ability to pay has fallen; government of all kinds is faced by

serious curtailment of income; the means of exchange are frozen in the currents of trade; the withered leaves of industrial enterprise lie on every side; farmers find no markets for their produce; the savings of many years in thousands of families are gone.

[3] More important, a host of unemployed citizens face the grim problem of existence, and an equally great number toil with little return. Only a foolish optimist can deny the dark realities of the moment.

[4] Yet our distress comes from no failure of substance. We are stricken by no plague of locusts. Compared with the perils which our forefathers conquered because they believed and were not afraid, we have still much to be thankful for. Nature still offers her bounty and human efforts have multiplied it. Plenty is at our doorstep, but a generous use of it languishes in the very sight of the supply. Primarily this is because the rulers of the exchange of mankind's goods have failed, through their own stubbornness and their own incompetence, have admitted their failure, and abdicated. Practices of the unscrupulous money changers stand indicted in the court of public opinion, rejected by the hearts and minds of men.

[5] True they have tried, but their efforts have been cast in the pattern of an outworn tradition. Faced by failure of credit they

have proposed only the lending of more money. Stripped of the lure of profit by which to induce our people to follow their false leadership, they have resorted to exhortations, pleading tearfully for restored confidence. They know only the rules of a generation of self-seekers. They have no vision, and when there is no vision the people perish.

[6] The money changers have fled from their high seats in the temple of our civilization. We may now restore that temple to the ancient truths. The measure of the restoration lies in the extent to which we apply social values more noble than mere monetary profit.

[7] Happiness lies not in the mere possession of money; it lies in the joy of achievement, in the thrill of creative effort. The joy and moral stimulation of work no longer must be forgotten in the mad chase of evanescent profits. These dark days will be worth all they cost us if they teach us that our true destiny is not to be ministered unto but to minister to ourselves and to our fellow men.

[8] Recognition of the falsity of material wealth as the standard of success goes hand in hand with the abandonment of the false belief that public office and high political position are to be valued only by the standards of pride of place and personal profit; and there must be an end to a conduct in banking and in business

which too often has given to a sacred trust the likeness of callous and selfish wrongdoing. Small wonder that confidence languishes, for it thrives only on honesty, on honor, on the sacredness of obligations, on faithful protection, on unselfish performance; without them it cannot live.

[9]   Restoration calls, however, not for changes in ethics alone. This Nation asks for action, and action now.

[10]   Our greatest primary task is to put people to work. This is no unsolvable problem if we face it wisely and courageously. It can be accomplished in part by direct recruiting by the Government itself, treating the task as we would treat the emergency of a war, but at the same time, through this employment, accomplishing greatly needed projects to stimulate and reorganize the use of our natural resources.

. . .

[11]   We face the arduous days that lie before us in the warm courage of the national unity; with the clear consciousness of seeking old and precious moral values; with the clean satisfaction that comes from the stem performance of duty by old and young alike. We aim at the assurance of a rounded and permanent national life.

[12] We do not distrust the future of essential democracy. The people of the United States have not failed. In their need they have registered a mandate that they want direct, vigorous action. They have asked for discipline and direction under leadership. They have made me the present instrument of their wishes. In the spirit of the gift I take it.

[13] In this dedication of a Nation we humbly ask the blessing of God. May He protect each and every one of us. May He guide me in the days to come.

(Photo by Getty Images)

I. この演説の内容について，以下に答えなさい。

　A.　第2パラグラフ1行目の "In such a spirit on my part" とは，どのような精神か，第1パラグラフのなかから，最も適切なセンテンスを抜き出し，日本語でその意味するところを簡潔に答えなさい。

　B.　第2パラグラフ1行目の "In such a spirit ... on yours" とは，どのような精神か，第1パラグラフのなかから，最も適切なセンテンスを抜き出し，日本語でその意味するところを簡潔に答えなさい。

　C.　ローズヴェルトは，大恐慌を誰の責任であると述べているか，それを最も直接的に言い表したセンテンスを第4パラグラフから抜き出し，日本語でその意味するところを簡潔に答えなさい。

　D.　ローズヴェルト大統領は金銭的な富よりも大切なものはなんであると述べているか，第6パラグラフから，最も適切な語句を抜き出し，日本語でその意味するところを簡潔に答えなさい。

II. 次の一節について，最善の日本語訳を作成してみてください。

So, first of all, let me assert my firm belief that the only thing we have to fear is fear itself — nameless, unreasoning, unjustified terror which paralyzes needed efforts to convert retreat into advance. In every dark hour of our national life a leadership of frankness and vigor has met with that understanding and support of the people themselves which is essential to victory.

III. 辞書を読み，次の5つの単語がどのような意味をとりうるかを理
解しましょう。

shrink

Nor need we **shrink** from honestly facing conditions in our country
today.

Values have **shrunken** to fantastic levels.

endure

This great Nation will **endure** as it has endured, will revive and will
prosper.

assert

Let me **assert** my firm belief that the only thing we have to fear is
fear itself.

convince, critical

I am **convinced** that you will again give that support to leadership
in these **critical** days.

admit

They have **admitted** their failure.

発展的課題

A. フランクリン・D・ローズヴェルト大統領の政治は,「ニューディール」政策として知られます。ニューディールの主張する「新しさ」とは,どのような新しさだったのでしょうか。この演説の中で用いられている,新旧の対比に注目しながら論じなさい。

B. ローズヴェルト大統領は,この演説の中で,大恐慌という一見解決不可能な経済問題を,誰もが賛成しうる道徳論に巧みに置き換えています。どこで,どのような言葉遣いによってその転換を行っているか,分析しなさい。

C. "The only thing we have to fear is fear itself." という有名な一節は,どの段階で誰によって書き加えられたか,放送授業のなかでのフランクリン・D・ローズヴェルト図書館博物館のポール・スパロー館長へのインタビューに基づいて答えなさい(インタビュー全文テクストは,システム WAKABA で参照できます)。

Chapter 5 | Franklin D. Roosevelt's First Fireside Chat (1933)

〈Photo by Getty Images〉

　フランクリン・D・ローズヴェルト大統領が最初に取り組まなければなら
なかった課題は，銀行危機の克服だった。1929年と1931年の預金取り付け
パニックにより4000の銀行が閉鎖され，1933年にはその数は9000に昇って
いた。ローズヴェルト大統領は就任と同時に，銀行休業（Banking Holiday）
を宣言し，銀行倒産を防止する。銀行を再開するにあたり，大統領はラジオ
のマイクの前に立ち，アメリカ国民に銀行預金を呼びかける。ローズヴェル
ト大統領は，炉端でラジオを聴いているごく普通のアメリカ人に向かって，
ささやきかけるかのような声で，親しく語りかけた。炉端講話は直ちに効果
を発揮し，アメリカ国民は再び銀行に預金をするようになった。

　ローズヴェルトが在任中行った30回の炉端講話は，政治演説における声の
あり方を大きく変えた。

[1] My friends, I want to talk for a few minutes with the people of the United States about banking — to talk with the comparatively few who understand the mechanics of banking, but more particularly with the overwhelming majority of you who use banks for the making of deposits and the drawing of checks. I want to tell you what has been done in the last few days, and why it was done, and what the next steps are going to be. I recognize that the many proclamations from the state capitals and from Washington, the legislation, the Treasury regulations and so forth, couched for the most part in banking and legal terms, ought to be explained for the benefit of the average citizen. I owe this in particular because of the fortitude and the good temper with which everybody has accepted the inconvenience and the hardships of the banking holiday. And I know that when you understand what we in Washington have been about I shall continue to have your cooperation as fully as I have had your sympathy and your help during the past week.

[2] First of all, let me state the simple fact that when you deposit money in a bank the bank does not put the money into a safe deposit vault. It invests your money in many different forms of credit — in bonds, in commercial paper, in mortgages, and in many other kinds of loans. In other words, the bank puts your money to work to keep the wheels of industry and of agriculture turning round. A comparatively small part of the money that you put into the bank is kept in currency — an amount which in

normal times is wholly sufficient to cover the cash needs of the average citizen. In other words, the total amount of all the currency in the country is only a comparatively small proportion of the total deposits in all the banks of the country.

[3] What, then, happened during the last few days of February and the first few days of March? Because of undermined confidence on the part of the public, there was a general rush by a large portion of our population to turn bank deposits into currency or gold — a rush so great that the soundest banks couldn't get enough currency to meet the demand. The reason for this was that on the spur of the moment it was, of course, impossible to sell perfectly sound assets of a bank and convert them into cash except at panic prices far below their real value.

[4] By the afternoon of March 3, a week ago last Friday, scarcely a bank in the country was open to do business. Proclamations closing them in whole or in part had been issued by the governors in almost all of the states.

[5] It was then that I issued the proclamation providing for the national bank holiday, and this was the first step in the government's reconstruction of our financial and economic fabric.

. . .

[6] It is possible that when the banks resume a very few people who have not recovered from their fear may again begin withdrawals. Let me make it clear to you that the banks will take care of all needs except of course the hysterical demands of hoarders — and it is my belief that hoarding during the past week has become an exceedingly unfashionable pastime in every part of our nation. It needs no prophet to tell you that when the people find that they can get their money — that they can get it when they want it for all legitimate purposes — the phantom of fear will soon be laid. People will again be glad to have their money where it will be safely taken care of and where they can use it conveniently at any time. I can assure you, my friends, that it is safer to keep your money in a reopened bank than it is to keep it under the mattress.

[7] The success of our whole national program depends, of course, on the cooperation of the public — on its intelligent support and its use of a reliable system.

[8] Remember that the essential accomplishment of the new legislation is that it makes it possible for banks more readily to convert their assets into cash than was the case before. More liberal provision has been made for banks to borrow on these assets at the reserve banks and more liberal provision has also been made for issuing currency on the security of these good assets. This currency is not fiat currency. It is issued only on

adequate security, and every good bank has an abundance of such security.

[9] One more point before I close. There will be, of course, some banks unable to reopen without being reorganized. The new law allows the government to assist in making these reorganizations quickly and effectively and even allows the government to subscribe to at least a part of any new capital that may be required.

[10] I hope you can see, my friends, from this essential recital of what your government is doing that there is nothing complex, nothing radical, in the process.

[11] We had a bad banking situation. Some of our bankers had shown themselves either incompetent or dishonest in their handling of the people's funds. They had used the money entrusted to them in speculations and unwise loans. This was, of course, not true in the vast majority of our banks, but it was true in enough of them to shock the people of the United States for a time into a sense of insecurity and to put them into a frame of mind where they did not differentiate, but seemed to assume that the acts of a comparative few had tainted them all. And so it became the government's job to straighten out this situation and to do it as quickly as possible. And that job is being performed.

[12] I do not promise you that every bank will be reopened or that individual losses will not be suffered, but there will be no losses that possibly could be avoided; and there would have been more and greater losses had we continued to drift. I can even promise you salvation for some at least of the sorely pressed banks. We shall be engaged not merely in reopening sound banks but in the creation of more sound banks through reorganization.

[13] It has been wonderful to me to catch the note of confidence from all over the country. I can never be sufficiently grateful to the people for the loyal support that they have given me in their acceptance of the judgment that has dictated our course, even though all our processes may not have seemed clear to them.

[14] After all, there is an element in the readjustment of our financial system more important than currency, more important than gold, and that is the confidence of the people themselves. Confidence and courage are the essentials of success in carrying out our plan. You people must have faith; you must not be stampeded by rumors or guesses. Let us unite in banishing fear. We have provided the machinery to restore our financial system; and it is up to you to support and make it work.

[15] It is your problem, my friends, your problem no less than it is mine. Together we cannot fail.

I. この演説の内容について，以下に答えなさい。

　A. 預金者が一斉に預金の払い戻しを求めても銀行がそれに対応でき
　　　ない理由をわかりやすく説明したセンテンスを，第2パラグラフ
　　　から抜き出し，日本語でその意味するところを簡潔に説明しなさ
　　　い。

　B. 取り付け騒動のメカニズムをわかりやすく説明しているのはどの
　　　パラグラフですか。それに基づいて，取り付け騒動とは何かを日
　　　本語で簡潔に答えなさい。

　C. ローズヴェルト大統領は，お金より大切なものは何だと述べてい
　　　ますか。最も適切なセンテンスを抜き出し，日本語でその意味す
　　　るところを簡潔に説明しなさい。

II. 次の一節について，最善の日本語訳を作成してみてください。

　It needs no prophet to tell you that when the people find that
they can get their money — that they can get it when they want
it for all legitimate purposes — the phantom of fear will soon be
laid. People will again be glad to have their money where it will
be safely taken care of and where they can use it conveniently at
any time. I can assure you, my friends, that it is safer to keep
your money in a reopened bank than it is to keep it under the
mattress.

III. 辞書を読み，次の5つの単語がどのような意味をとりうるかを理解しましょう。

deposit

People use banks for the making of **deposits** and the drawing of checks.

When you **deposit** money in a bank the bank does not put the money into a safe deposit vault.

currency

A comparatively small part of the money that you put into the bank is kept in **currency** — an amount which in normal times is wholly sufficient to cover the cash needs of the average citizen.

The total amount of all the **currency** in the country is only a comparatively small proportion of the total **deposits** in all the banks of the country.

meet

The soundest banks couldn't get enough **currency** to **meet** the demand.

issue

I **issued** the proclamation providing for the national bank holiday.

This **currency** is ... **issued** only on adequate security, and every good bank has an abundance of such security.

asset

Banks converted their **assets** into cash.

More liberal provision has also been made for **issuing currency** on the security of these good **assets**.

発展的課題

A. ローズヴェルト大統領は，なぜ通常の演説ではなく，ラジオによる炉端講話（fireside chat）というかたちで国民に伝えることを選択したか，考えてみましょう。

B. ローズヴェルト大統領の就任演説とこの炉端講話を比較し，声の発し方やトーンの違いについて述べなさい。

C. 上流階級出身の大統領は，なぜ貧しい一般国民の苦しみに共感し近しく語りかけることができたのか，放送授業のなかでのポール・スパロー館長へのインタビューに基づいて答えなさい（インタビュー全文テクストは，システム WAKABA で参照できます）。

（Photo by Getty Images）

Chapter 6 | Eleanor Roosevelt's Speech on Human Rights (1951)

〈Photo by Getty Images〉

　アメリカ合衆国には，まだ女性の大統領が登場していないが，それに最も近い存在は，エレノア・ローズヴェルトであった。エレノアは，シオドア・ローズヴェルトの姪であり，フランクリン・D・ローズヴェルト大統領の妻である。

　エレノアは，一般民衆のためにたゆまず権力と戦うというシオドア・ローズヴェルトの信念を引き継ぎ，ソーシャルワーカーとして貧しい階層の子どもたちの教育に携わり，大統領夫人となってからもこれを続けた。ニューディール政策のなかの最も進歩的な部分は，エレノアが夫に与えた強い影響力によるものとされる。

　フランクリン・D・ローズヴェルト大統領の死去の後，エレノアは国連人権委員会の座長を務め，冷戦の影の迫る困難な状況のなかで，世界人権宣言を取りまとめる。1948年12月10日午前3時，世界人権宣言はようやく全会一致で採択される。国連総会の会場で，全員が起立しエレノア・ローズヴェルトに拍手を送った。

[1] I'm very glad to be able to take part in this celebration in St. Louis on Human Rights Day. Ever since the declaration of human rights, the Universal Declaration of Human Rights, was passed in Paris in 1948 on December the 10th, we have fostered the observance of this day not only in the United States but throughout the world.

(Photo by Getty Images)

[2] The object is to make people everywhere conscious of the importance of human rights and freedoms.

[3] The reason for that is that these are spoken of and emphasized in the Charter of the United Nations, and the declaration was written to elaborate the rights already mentioned in the charter and to emphasize also, for all of us, the fact that the building of human rights would be one of the foundation stones, on which we would build in the world, an atmosphere in which peace can grow.

[4] For that reason, all over the world we've encouraged the Association for the United Nations to observe a whole week before United Nations Day comes around to explain the United Nations and what goes on in that organization and when we

come to the celebration for human rights we try to particularly have people study the declaration so that they will really understand what were considered to be the most essential rights for all people to have throughout the world.

[5]   They fall into different groups and one reason that we are now considering the writing of a covenant or covenants is because we feel that these rights should sometimes be actually written into the laws of countries throughout the world, and that can be done by the adoption of covenants and the changing of laws to meet whatever a country has accepted in a covenant which will be written in treaty form.

[6]   These things must be well understood because even though you pass, you accept treaties and countries ratify those treaties, the real change, which must give to people throughout the world their human rights, must come about in the hearts of people.

[7]   We must want our fellow human beings to have rights and freedoms which give them dignity and which will give them a sense that they are human beings that can walk the earth with their heads high and look all men in the face.

[8]   If we observe these rights, for ourselves and for others, I think we will find that it is easier in the world to build peace because war destroys all human rights and freedoms, so in fighting for those we fight for peace.

72

I. この演説の内容について，以下に答えなさい。

  A. 人権週間の目的を分かりやすく説明したセンテンスを抜き出し，日本語でその意味するところを簡潔に説明しなさい。

  B. エレノア・ローズヴェルトは，国連憲章と世界人権宣言とのあいだの関係をどのように説明していますか。最も適切なセンテンスを抜き出し，日本語でその意味するところを簡潔に説明しなさい。

  C. エレノア・ローズヴェルトは，人権と平和とのあいだの関係をどのように説明していますか。最も適切なセンテンスを抜き出し，日本語でその意味するところを簡潔に説明しなさい。

II. 次の一節について，最善の日本語訳を作成してみてください。

We must want our fellow human beings to have rights and freedoms which give them dignity and which will give them a sense that they are human beings that can walk the earth with their heads high and look all men in the face.

III. 辞書を読み，次の5つの単語がどのような意味をとりうるかを理解しましょう。

foster, observe

We have **fostered** the **observance** of this day not only in the United States but throughout the world.

If we **observe** these rights, for ourselves and for others, I think we will find that it is easier in the world to build peace.

elaborate

The declaration was written to **elaborate** the rights already mentioned in the charter.

encourage

We've **encouraged** the Association for the United Nations to **observe** a whole week before United Nations Day comes around.

adopt

That can be done by the **adoption** of covenants and the changing of laws.

発展的課題

A. 戦争および平和に対するエレノア・ローズヴェルトの考え方を，シオドア・ローズヴェルトの考え方と比較しなさい。

B. 世界人権宣言については，その法的拘束力について論議が続いています。どのような問題が生じうるか，この演説のテクストに即して考えてみましょう。

C. この演説の組み立てや言葉遣いを利用して日本の記念日（例えば憲法記念日や体育の日）の意義を説明する英文を書いてみましょう。

D. 放送授業のなかでのローズヴェルト夫妻の夫婦関係がどのようなものであったか，ポール・スパロー館長へのインタビューやその他の資料を手がかりに，あなた自身の考えを述べなさい（インタビュー全文テクストは，システム WAKABA で参照できます）。

Chapter 7 | Harry Truman's "Truman Doctrine" Speech (1947)

（Photo by Getty Images）

　第二次世界大戦終結を間近に，フランクリン・D・ローズヴェルト大統領は病死し，比較的知名度の低かったハリー・S・トルーマン副大統領が大統領に就任する。トルーマン大統領のもとで，アメリカは広島・長崎に原爆を投下し，大戦に勝利し，そして半世紀にわたる東西冷戦の時代に突入していく。

　トルーマン大統領は，ギリシャで起こった中道右派政権と共産党とのあいだの内戦に介入し，反共産主義勢力に対して軍事的経済的な支援を行うことを決め，1947 年 3 月 12 日，議会の両院合同会議（Joint Congress）で演説を行う。この演説は「トルーマン・ドクトリン」として知られる。

　トルーマン大統領は，この演説のなかで，その後およそ半世紀に及ぶ東西冷戦の歴史と世界地図を形作ったと言っても過言ではないだろう。

[1] At the present moment in world history nearly every nation must choose between alternative ways of life. The choice is too often not a free one. One way of life is based upon the will of the majority, and is distinguished by free institutions, representative government, free elections, guarantees of individual liberty, freedom of speech and religion, and freedom from political oppression. The second way of life is based upon the will of a minority forcibly imposed upon the majority. It relies upon terror and oppression, a controlled press and radio, fixed elections, and the suppression of personal freedoms.

[2] I believe that it must be the policy of the United States to support free peoples who are resisting attempted subjugation by armed minorities or by outside pressures.

[3] I believe that we must assist free peoples to work out their own destinies in their own way.

[4] I believe that our help should be primarily through economic and financial aid which is essential to economic stability and orderly political processes.

[5] The world is not static, and the status quo is not sacred. But we cannot allow changes in the status quo in violation of the Charter of the United Nations by such methods as coercion, or by such subterfuges as political infiltration. In helping free and

independent nations to maintain their freedom, the United States will be giving effect to the principles of the Charter of the United Nations.

[6]   It is necessary only to glance at a map to realize that the survival and integrity of the Greek nation are of grave importance in a much wider situation. If Greece should fall under the control of an armed minority, the effect upon its neighbor, Turkey, would be immediate and serious. Confusion and disorder might well spread throughout the entire Middle East. Moreover, the disappearance of Greece as an independent state would have a profound effect upon those countries in Europe whose peoples are struggling against great difficulties to maintain their freedoms and their independence while they repair the damages of war.

[7]   It would be an unspeakable tragedy if these countries, which have struggled so long against overwhelming odds, should lose that victory for which they sacrificed so much. Collapse of free institutions and loss of independence would be disastrous not only for them but for the world. Discouragement and possibly failure would quickly be the lot of neighboring peoples striving to maintain their freedom and independence.

[8]   Should we fail to aid Greece and Turkey in this fateful hour, the effect will be far reaching to the West as well as to the East.

[9] We must take immediate and resolute action. I therefore ask the Congress to provide authority for assistance to Greece and Turkey in the amount of $400,000,000 for the period ending June 30, 1948. In requesting these funds, I have taken into consideration the maximum amount of relief assistance which would be furnished to Greece out of the $350,000,000 which I recently requested that the Congress authorize for the prevention of starvation and suffering in countries devastated by the war.

[10] In addition to funds, I ask the Congress to authorize the detail of American civilian and military personnel to Greece and Turkey, at the request of those countries, to assist in the tasks of reconstruction, and for the purpose of supervising the use of such financial and material assistance as may be furnished. I recommend that authority also be provided for the instruction and training of selected Greek and Turkish personnel. Finally, I ask that the Congress provide authority which will permit the speediest and most effective use, in terms of needed commodities, supplies, and equipment, of such funds as may be authorized. If further funds, or further authority, should be needed for the purposes indicated in this message, I shall not hesitate to bring the situation before the Congress. On this subject the Executive and Legislative branches of the Government must work together.

[11] This is a serious course upon which we embark. I would not

recommend it except that the alternative is much more serious. The United States contributed $341,000,000,000 toward winning World War II. This is an investment in world freedom and world peace. The assistance that I am recommending for Greece and Turkey amounts to little more than 1 tenth of 1 percent of this investment. It is only common sense that we should safeguard this investment and make sure that it was not in vain. The seeds of totalitarian regimes are nurtured by misery and want. They spread and grow in the evil soil of poverty and strife. They reach their full growth when the hope of a people for a better life has died.

[12] We must keep that hope alive.

[13] The free peoples of the world look to us for support in maintaining their freedoms. If we falter in our leadership, we may endanger the peace of the world. And we shall surely endanger the welfare of this nation.

[14] Great responsibilities have been placed upon us by the swift movement of events. I am confident that the Congress will face these responsibilities squarely.

(Photo by Getty Images)

I. この演説の内容について，以下に答えなさい。

A. 第1パラグラフで，トルーマン大統領は世界を2つの体制に分ける二分論を展開しています。どのような体制とどのような体制か，日本語で簡潔に説明しなさい。

B. この演説は，いわゆる「ドミノ理論」，つまりある一国が共産主義化すればドミノ倒しのように共産主義は隣接する国々に波及するという考え方の，最初の表れの1つであるとされています。ドミノ理論が展開されているパラグラフを指摘し，日本語で分かりやすく要約しなさい。

C. 貧困と全体主義とのあいだの関係を説明したパラグラフを指摘し，そのなかから最も端的に主張を言い表したセンテンスを抜き出し，その意味するところを簡潔に日本語で説明しなさい。

D. 演説の終わりの方で，トルーマン大統領はアメリカ合衆国にはどのような責任があると述べていますか。最も適切なセンテンスを抜き出し，その意味するところを簡潔に日本語で説明しなさい。

II. 次の一節について，最善の日本語訳を作成してみてください。

The assistance that I am recommending for Greece and Turkey amounts to little more than 1 tenth of 1 percent of this investment. It is only common sense that we should safeguard this investment and make sure that it was not in vain. The seeds of totalitarian regimes are nurtured by misery and want. They spread and grow in the evil soil of poverty and strife. They reach their full growth when the hope of a people for a better life has died.

III. 辞書を読み，次の5つの単語がどのような意味をとりうるかを理解しましょう。

alternative
Nearly every nation must choose between **alternative** ways of life.
The **alternative** is much more serious.

institution
One way of life is based upon the will of the majority, and is distinguished by free **institutions**, representative government, free elections, guarantees of individual liberty, freedom of speech and religion, and freedom from political oppression.
Collapse of free **institutions** and loss of independence would be disastrous not only for them but for the world.

impose
The will of a minority forcibly **imposed** upon the majority.

executive
On this subject the **Executive** and Legislative branches of the Government must work together.

embark
This is a serious course upon which we **embark**.

A. 「トルーマン・ドクトリン」は，ドミノ理論の端緒とされ，今日ではドミノ理論は誤謬あるいは詭弁に基づくものだったとする見解があります。この演説のなかで展開されている論理のなかに誤謬・詭弁があるとすると，それはどこに見られるか，具体的に指摘しなさい。

B. この演説のなかに "communism" という言葉が1回も出てこないのはなぜでしょうか。また共産主義は，ほかのどのような語彙や概念に置き換えられているか指摘しなさい。

C. この演説のなかで語られている「平和」と，前章でエレノア・ローズヴェルトが語っている「平和」，そしてこのあとチャプター9でケネディ大統領が語っている「平和」を比較し，それらのあいだの共通点と相違について論じなさい。

Chapter 8 | John F. Kennedy's Cuban Missile Crisis Speech (1962)

(Photo by Getty Images)

1962年10月14日，アメリカ合衆国は偵察機が撮影した航空写真から，ソビエト連邦（当時）がキューバに密かに核ミサイル基地を建設しつつあることを突き止める。米ソの対立によって，世界は全面核戦争の一歩手前にまで危機が高まる。

このような危機的状況のなかで，10月22日午後7時，ジョン・F・ケネディ大統領は，ホワイト・ハウスの執務室から，全米に向けてテレビ演説を行った。

[1] Good evening my fellow citizens:

[2] This Government, as promised, has maintained the closest surveillance of the Soviet Military buildup on the island of Cuba. Within the past week, unmistakable evidence has established the fact that a series of offensive missile sites is now in preparation on that imprisoned island. The purpose of these bases can be none other than to provide a nuclear strike capability against the Western Hemisphere.

[3] Upon receiving the first preliminary hard information of this nature last Tuesday morning at 9 a.m., I directed that our surveillance be stepped up. And having now confirmed and completed our evaluation of the evidence and our decision on a course of action, this Government feels obliged to report this new crisis to you in fullest detail.

[4] The characteristics of these new missile sites indicate two distinct types of installations. Several of them include medium range ballistic missiles capable of carrying a nuclear warhead for a distance of more than 1,000 nautical miles. Each of these missiles, in short, is capable of striking Washington, D.C., the Panama Canal, Cape Canaveral, Mexico City, or any other city in the southeastern part of the United States, in Central America, or in the Caribbean area.

[5]   Additional sites not yet completed appear to be designed for intermediate range ballistic missiles — capable of traveling more than twice as far — and thus capable of striking most of the major cities in the Western Hemisphere, ranging as far north as Hudson Bay, Canada, and as far south as Lima, Peru. In addition, jet bombers, capable of carrying nuclear weapons, are now being uncrated and assembled in Cuba, while the necessary air bases are being prepared.

[6]   This urgent transformation of Cuba into an important strategic base — by the presence of these large, long range, and clearly offensive weapons of sudden mass destruction — constitutes an explicit threat to the peace and security of all the Americas, in flagrant and deliberate defiance of the Rio Pact of 1947, the traditions of this Nation and hemisphere, the joint resolution of the 87th Congress, the Charter of the United Nations, and my own public warnings to the Soviets on September 4 and 13. This action also contradicts the repeated assurances of Soviet spokesmen, both publicly and privately delivered, that the arms buildup in Cuba would

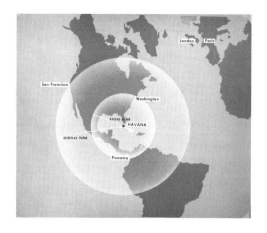

retain its original defensive character, and that the Soviet Union had no need or desire to station strategic missiles on the territory of any other nation.

. . .

[7] This Nation is prepared to present its case against the Soviet threat to peace, and our own proposals for a peaceful world, at any time and in any forum — in the OAS, in the United Nations, or in any other meeting that could be useful — without limiting our freedom of action. We have in the past made strenuous efforts to limit the spread of nuclear weapons. We have proposed the elimination of all arms and military bases in a fair and effective disarmament treaty. We are prepared to discuss new proposals for the removal of tensions on both sides — including the possibility of a genuinely independent Cuba, free to determine its own destiny. We have no wish to war with the Soviet Union — for we are a peaceful people who desire to live in peace with all other peoples.

[8] But it is difficult to settle or even discuss these problems in an atmosphere of intimidation. That is why this latest Soviet threat — or any other threat which is made either independently or in response to our actions this week — must and will be met with determination. Any hostile move anywhere in the world against the safety and freedom of peoples to whom we are

committed — including in particular the brave people of West Berlin — will be met by whatever action is needed.

[9] Finally, I want to say a few words to the captive people of Cuba, to whom this speech is being directly carried by special radio facilities. I speak to you as a friend, as one who knows of your deep attachment to your fatherland, as one who shares your aspirations for liberty and justice for all. And I have watched and the American people have watched with deep sorrow how your nationalist revolution was betrayed — and how your fatherland fell under foreign domination. Now your leaders are no longer Cuban leaders inspired by Cuban ideals. They are puppets and agents of an international conspiracy which has turned Cuba against your friends and neighbors in the Americas — and turned it into the first Latin American country to become a target for nuclear war — the first Latin American country to have these weapons on its soil.

[10] These new weapons are not in your interest. They contribute nothing to your peace and well-being. They can only undermine it. But this country has no wish to cause you to suffer or to impose any system upon you. We know that your lives and land are being used as pawns by those who deny your freedom.

[11] Many times in the past, the Cuban people have risen to throw out tyrants who destroyed their liberty. And I have no

doubt that most Cubans today look forward to the time when they will be truly free — free from foreign domination, free to choose their own leaders, free to select their own system, free to own their own land, free to speak and write and worship without fear or degradation. And then shall Cuba be welcomed back to the society of free nations and to the associations of this hemisphere.

[12] My fellow citizens: let no one doubt that this is a difficult and dangerous effort on which we have set out. No one can see precisely what course it will take or what costs or casualties will be incurred. Many months of sacrifice and self-discipline lie ahead — months in which our patience and our will will be tested — months in which many threats and denunciations will keep us aware of our dangers. But the greatest danger of all would be to do nothing.

[13] The path we have chosen for the present is full of hazards, as all paths are — but it is the one most consistent with our character and courage as a nation and our commitments around the world. The cost of freedom is always high — and Americans have always paid it. And one path we shall never choose, and that is the path of surrender or submission.

[14] Our goal is not the victory of might, but the vindication of right — not peace at the expense of freedom, but both peace and

freedom, here in this hemisphere, and, we hope, around the world. God willing, that goal will be achieved.

[15] Thank you and good night.

(Photo by Getty Images)

I. この演説の内容について，以下に答えなさい。

A. このテレビ演説の目的を最も簡潔明瞭に示したセンテンスを抜き出し，日本語でその意味するところを簡潔に説明しなさい。

B. アメリカ国民がどのような危機に直面しているかを最も具体的に示したセンテンスを抜き出し，日本語でその意味するところを簡潔に説明しなさい。

C. キューバ国民に語りかけているのは，第何パラグラフから第何パラグラフですか。そのなかでキューバ国民への最も重要なメッセージとなっているセンテンスを抜き出し，日本語でその意味するところを簡潔に説明しなさい。

D. ケネディ大統領の，ミサイル危機に臨む姿勢を最も端的に示したセンテンスを抜き出し，日本語でその意味するところを簡潔に説明しなさい。

II. 次の一節について，最善の日本語訳を作成してみてください。

The path we have chosen for the present is full of hazards, as all paths are — but it is the one most consistent with our character and courage as a nation and our commitments around the world. The cost of freedom is always high — and Americans have always paid it. And one path we shall never choose, and that is the path of surrender or submission.

Our goal is not the victory of might, but the vindication of right — not peace at the expense of freedom, but both peace and freedom, here in this hemisphere, and, we hope, around the world. God willing, that goal will be achieved.

Thank you and good night.

III. 辞書を読み，次の6つの単語がどのような意味をとりうるかを理解しましょう。

establish

Unmistakable evidence has **established** the fact that a series of offensive missile sites is now in preparation.

oblige

This Government feels **obliged** to report this new crisis to you in fullest detail.

We are obliged to prepare for the class.

indicate

The characteristics of these new missile sites **indicate** two distinct types of installations.

interest

These new weapons are not in your **interest**.

commit, consistent

The path we have chosen for the present is full of hazards, as all paths are — but it is the one most **consistent** with our character and courage as a nation and our **commitments** around the world.

発展的課題

A. この演説のなかで，"the Western Hemisphere" という表現が繰り返されているのはなぜでしょうか。

B. この演説のなかで，アメリカ合衆国の国民性をどのように性格づけているか，具体的表現を抜き出しながら論じなさい。

C. 演説の後半で，キューバ国民への語りかけというかたちをとっているのはなぜでしょうか。それをふくめることは，アメリカの視聴者にとってどのような意味を持ちえたでしょうか。

Chapter 9 | John F. Kennedy's American University Commencement Address (1963)

（Photo by Getty Images）

　キューバ・ミサイル危機の翌年となる 1963 年の 6 月 10 日，ケネディ大統
領はアメリカン大学の卒業式に招かれて演説する。

　大統領や著名人を卒業式に招くのは，アメリカの大学の慣例であり，また
数々の歴史的名演説が大学の卒業式において残されている。そうしたなかに
あっても，「平和の戦略（strategy of peace）」についてのケネディ大統領の
演説は傑出した存在である。

　この年の 11 月，ケネディ大統領はダラスで暗殺者の凶弾に倒れる。

[1] President Anderson, members of the faculty, board of trustees, distinguished guests, my old colleague, Senator Bob Byrd, who has earned his degree through many years of attending night law school, while I am earning mine in the next 30 minutes, distinguished guests, ladies and gentlemen:

. . .

[2] "There are few earthly things more beautiful than a university," wrote John Masefield in his tribute to English universities — and his words are equally true today. He did not refer to spires and towers, to campus greens and ivied walls. He admired the splendid beauty of the university, he said, because it was "a place where those who hate ignorance may strive to know, where those who perceive truth may strive to make others see."

[3] I have, therefore, chosen this time and this place to discuss a topic on which ignorance too often abounds and the truth is too rarely perceived — yet it is the most important topic on earth: world peace.

[4] What kind of peace do I mean? What kind of peace do we seek? Not a Pax Americana enforced on the world by American weapons of war. Not the peace of the grave or the security of the slave. I am talking about genuine peace, the kind of peace that

makes life on earth worth living, the kind that enables men and nations to grow and to hope and to build a better life for their children — not merely peace for Americans but peace for all men and women — not merely peace in our time but peace for all time.

[5] I speak of peace because of the new face of war. Total war makes no sense in an age when great powers can maintain large and relatively invulnerable nuclear forces and refuse to surrender without resort to those forces. It makes no sense in an age when a single nuclear weapon contains almost ten times the explosive force delivered by all the allied air forces in the Second World War. It makes no sense in an age when the deadly poisons produced by a nuclear exchange would be carried by wind and water and soil and seed to the far corners of the globe and to generations yet unborn.

[6] Today the expenditure of billions of dollars every year on weapons acquired for the purpose of making sure we never need to use them is essential to keeping the peace. But surely the acquisition of such idle stockpiles — which can only destroy and never create — is not the only, much less the most efficient, means of assuring peace.

[7] I speak of peace, therefore, as the necessary rational end of rational men. I realize that the pursuit of peace is not as dramatic

as the pursuit of war — and frequently the words of the pursuer fall on deaf ears. But we have no more urgent task.

[8] Some say that it is useless to speak of world peace or world law or world disarmament — and that it will be useless until the leaders of the Soviet Union adopt a more enlightened attitude. I hope they do. I believe we can help them do it. But I also believe that we must reexamine our own attitude — as individuals and as a Nation — for our attitude is as essential as theirs. And every graduate of this school, every thoughtful citizen who despairs of war and wishes to bring peace, should begin by looking inward — by examining his own attitude toward the possibilities of peace, toward the Soviet Union, toward the course of the cold war and toward freedom and peace here at home.

[9] First: Let us examine our attitude toward peace itself. Too many of us think it is impossible. Too many think it unreal. But that is a dangerous, defeatist belief. It leads to the conclusion that war is inevitable — that mankind is doomed — that we are gripped by forces we cannot control.

[10] We need not accept that view. Our problems are manmade — therefore, they can be solved by man. And man can be as big as he wants. No problem of human destiny is beyond human beings. Man's reason and spirit have often solved the seemingly unsolvable — and we believe they can do it again.

[11] I am not referring to the absolute, infinite concept of peace and good will of which some fantasies and fanatics dream. I do not deny the value of hopes and dreams but we merely invite discouragement and incredulity by making that our only and immediate goal.

[12] Let us focus instead on a more practical, more attainable peace — based not on a sudden revolution in human nature but on a gradual evolution in human institutions — on a series of concrete actions and effective agreements which are in the interest of all concerned. There is no single, simple key to this peace — no grand or magic formula to be adopted by one or two powers. Genuine peace must be the product of many nations, the sum of many acts. It must be dynamic, not static, changing to meet the challenge of each new generation. For peace is a process — a way of solving problems.

[13] With such a peace, there will still be quarrels and conflicting interests, as there are within families and nations. World peace, like community peace, does not require that each man love his neighbor — it requires only that they live together in mutual tolerance, submitting their disputes to a just and peaceful settlement. And history teaches us that enmities between nations, as between individuals, do not last forever. However fixed our likes and dislikes may seem, the tide of time and events will often bring surprising changes in the relations between

98

nations and neighbors.

[14] So let us persevere. Peace need not be impracticable, and war need not be inevitable. By defining our goal more clearly, by making it seem more manageable and less remote, we can help all peoples to see it, to draw hope from it, and to move irresistibly toward it.

. . .

[15] The United States, as the world knows, will never start a war. We do not want a war. We do not now expect a war. This generation of Americans has already had enough — more than enough — of war and hate and oppression. We shall be prepared if others wish it. We shall be alert to try to stop it. But we shall also do our part to build a world of peace where the weak are safe and the strong are just. We are not helpless before that task or hopeless of its success. Confident and unafraid, we labor on — not toward a strategy of annihilation but toward a strategy of peace.

(Photo by Getty Images)

I. この演説の内容について，以下に答えなさい。

A. この演説のなかで，なぜあえて「平和」という論題を取り上げる
のか，その理由を最初に説明しているセンテンスを抜き出し，日
本語でその意味するところを簡潔に説明しなさい。

B. 米ソの核軍備競争の無意味さを批判したパラグラフを指摘し，そ
のなかで繰り返し用いられている言葉遣いを抜き出しなさい。

C. 第 10 ～ 13 パラグラフで，ケネディ大統領は「平和」に関する 2
つの理念を比較しています。本文から適切な語句を抜き出し，下
の表を完成させなさい。

absolute peace	concept	good will	sudden revolution	static
practical peace				

II. 次の一節について，最善の日本語訳を作成してみてください。

What kind of peace do I mean? What kind of a peace do we seek?
Not a Pax Americana enforced on the world by American
weapons of war. Not the peace of the grave or the security of the
slave. I am talking about genuine peace, the kind of peace that
makes life on earth worth living, the kind that enables men and
nations to grow and to hope and to build a better life for their
children ― not merely peace for Americans but peace for all men
and women ― not merely peace in our time but peace in all time.

III. 辞書を読み，次の6つの単語がどのような意味をとりうるかを理
解しましょう。

perceive

The university is a place where those who hate ignorance may
strive to know, where those who **perceive** truth may strive to make
others see.
The truth is too rarely **perceived**.

adopt

It will be useless until the leaders of the Soviet Union **adopt** a more
enlightened attitude.
There is no single, simple key to this peace — no grand or magic
formula to be **adopted** by one or two powers.

accept

We need not **accept** that view.

submit

They live together in mutual tolerance, **submitting** their disputes to
a just and peaceful settlement.

discourage

I do not deny the value of hopes and dreams but we merely invite
discouragement and incredulity by making that our only and
immediate goal.

発展的課題

A.　大学の卒業式という場で，それとは必ずしも直接結びつかない「平和」という大きなテーマを提示するために，ケネディ大統領はどのようにイントロを構成しているか指摘しなさい。

B.　I.C 以外に比較対照を用いながら論述を展開している箇所を指摘しなさい。

C.　この演説の特徴の1つとして，頭韻法（alliteration）が，しばしば指摘されます。頭韻法とは，*"sink or swim"* "I have a dream that my four little children will one day live in a nation where they will not be judged by the color of their skin but by the content of their character." のように，連続ないし近接する単語に同じ子音を繰り返す言葉遣いです。この演説のなかで，頭韻法が効果的に用いられている箇所を指摘しなさい。

D.　ケネディ大統領がここで提起している「平和」の理念に対する，補足ないし批判として，あなた自身の考えを述べなさい。

Chapter 10 | Lyndon B. Johnson's "The Great Society" Speech (1964)

（Photo by Getty Images）

　ケネディ大統領の暗殺後，副大統領から昇格して大統領に就任したリンド
ン・B・ジョンソンは，もっぱらヴェトナム戦争の悪夢とともに記憶される
ことになるが，同時に公民権法を成立させたリベラルな政治家でもあった。

　ケネディ暗殺の翌年となる，1964 年 5 月 22 日，ジョンソン大統領はミシ
ガン大学の卒業式で演説し，「偉大な社会（The Great Society)」というビジョ
ンを展開する。それはシオドア・ローズヴェルトの「ニュー・ナショナリズム」，
フランクリン・D・ローズヴェルトの「ニューディール」，そしてジョン・F・
ケネディの「ニュー・フロンティア」の系譜を引き継ぐ，「大きな政府」によ
るリベラルな社会の最後のビジョンだった。

[1] President Hatcher, Governor Romney, Senators McNamara and Hart, Congressmen Meader and Staebler, and other members of the fine Michigan delegation, members of the graduating class, my fellow Americans:

(Photo by Getty Images)

[2] It is a great pleasure to be here today. This university has been coeducational since 1870, but I do not believe it was on the basis of your accomplishments that a Detroit high school girl said, "In choosing a college, you first have to decide whether you want a coeducational school or an educational school."

[3] Well, we can find both here at Michigan, although perhaps at different hours.

[4] I came out here today very anxious to meet the Michigan student whose father told a friend of mine that his son's education had been a real value. It stopped his mother from bragging about him.

[5]   I have come today from the turmoil of your Capital to the tranquility of your campus to speak about the future of your country.

[6]   The purpose of protecting the life of our Nation and preserving the liberty of our citizens is to pursue the happiness of our people. Our success in that pursuit is the test of our success as a Nation. For a century we labored to settle and to subdue a continent. For half a century we called upon unbounded invention and untiring industry to create an order of plenty for all of our people.

[7]   The challenge of the next half century is whether we have the wisdom to use that wealth to enrich and elevate our national life, and to advance the quality of our American civilization.

[8]   Your imagination, your initiative, and your indignation will determine whether we build a society where progress is the servant of our needs, or a society where old values and new visions are buried under unbridled growth.

[9]   For in your time we have the opportunity to move not only toward the rich society and the powerful society, but upward to the Great Society.

[10] The Great Society rests on abundance and liberty for all. It demands an end to poverty and racial injustice, to which we are totally committed in our time. But that is just the beginning.

[11] The Great Society is a place where every child can find knowledge to enrich his mind and to enlarge his talents. It is a place where leisure is a welcome chance to build and reflect, not a feared cause of boredom and restlessness. It is a place where the city of man serves not only the needs of the body and the demands of commerce but the desire for beauty and the hunger for community.

[12] It is a place where man can renew contact with nature. It is a place which honors creation for its own sake and for what it adds to the understanding of the race. It is a place where men are more concerned with the quality of their goals than the quantity of their goods.

[13] But most of all, the Great Society is not a safe harbor, a resting place, a final objective, a finished work. It is a challenge constantly renewed, beckoning us toward a destiny where the meaning of our lives matches the marvelous products of our labor.

. . .

[14] While our Government has many programs directed at those issues, I do not pretend that we have the full answer to those problems.

[15] But I do promise this: We are going to assemble the best thought and the broadest knowledge from all over the world to find those answers for America. I intend to establish working groups to prepare a series of White House conferences and meetings — on the cities, on natural beauty, on the quality of education, and on other emerging challenges. And from these meetings and from this inspiration and from these studies we will begin to set our course toward the Great Society.

[16] The solution to these problems does not rest on a massive program in Washington, nor can it rely solely on the strained resources of local authority. They require us to create new concepts of cooperation, a creative federalism, between the National Capital and the leaders of local communities.

[17] Woodrow Wilson once wrote: "Every man sent out from his university should be a man of his Nation as well as a man of his time."

[18] Within your lifetime powerful forces, already loosed, will take us toward a way of life beyond the realm of our experience, almost beyond the bounds of our imagination.

[19] For better or for worse, your generation has been appointed by history to deal with those problems and to lead America toward a new age. You have the chance never before afforded to any people in any age. You can help build a society where the demands of morality, and the needs of the spirit, can be realized in the life of the Nation.

[20] So, will you join in the battle to give every citizen the full equality which God enjoins and the law requires, whatever his belief, or race, or the color of his skin?

[21] Will you join in the battle to give every citizen an escape from the crushing weight of poverty?

[22] Will you join in the battle to make it possible for all nations to live in enduring peace — as neighbors and not as mortal enemies?

[23] Will you join in the battle to build the Great Society, to prove that our material progress is only the foundation on which we will build a richer life of mind and spirit?

[24] There are those timid souls who say this battle cannot be won; that we are condemned to a soulless wealth. I do not agree. We have the power to shape the civilization that we want. But we need your will, your labor, and your hearts, if we are to build

that kind of society.

[25] Those who came to this land sought to build more than just a new country. They sought a new world. So I have come here today to your campus to say that you can make their vision our reality. So let us from this moment begin our work so that in the future men will look back and say: It was then, after a long and weary way, that man turned the exploits of his genius to the full enrichment of his life.

[26] Thank you. Good-bye.

(Photo by Getty Images)

110

I. この演説の内容について，以下に答えなさい。

  A. ジョンソン大統領は，演説の前半で，彼の「偉大な社会」というビジョンの要件を，4点挙げています。それぞれをできるだけ簡潔に日本語でまとめなさい。

  B. ジョンソン大統領は，演説の後半で，卒業生たちに「偉大な社会」の実現のために闘うことを呼びかけています。ジョンソンの4点の呼びかけを，それぞれできるだけ簡潔に日本語でまとめなさい。

  C. 古来，物質的な豊かさと精神的な豊かさは二律背反としてとらえられてきました。例えば日本には「ぼろは着てても心は錦」「清貧」といった言葉があり，英語には「天国にお金は持っていけない（You can't take it with you.）」という言い方があります。ジョンソン大統領は物質的な豊かさと精神的な豊かさとのあいだの関係をどのようにとらえていますか。それが最もわかりやすく表現されたセンテンスを抜き出し，その意味するところを簡潔に日本語で説明しなさい。

II. 次の一節について，最善の日本語訳を作成してみてください。

Will you join in the battle to build the Great Society, to prove that our material progress is only the foundation on which we will build a richer life of mind and spirit? There are those timid souls who say this battle cannot be won; that we are condemned to a soulless wealth. I do not agree. We have the power to shape the civilization that we want. But we need your will, your labor, and your hearts, if we are to build that kind of society.

III. 辞書を読み，次の6つの単語がどのような意味をとりうるかを理解しましょう。

advance

The challenge of the next half century is whether we have the wisdom to **advance** the quality of our American civilization.

initiative

Your imagination, your **initiative**, and your indignation will determine whether we build a society where progress is the servant of our needs, or a society where old values and new visions are buried under unbridled growth.

abundant

The Great Society rests on **abundance** and liberty for all.

commit

It demands an end to poverty and racial injustice, to which we are totally **committed** in our time.

assemble

We are going to **assemble** the best thought and the broadest knowledge from all over the world to find those answers for America.

112

afford

You have the chance never before **afforded** to any people in any age.

A. I.A で解答した，「偉大な社会」の 4 つの要件のうち，4 番目は他の 3 つとやや性質が異なるものになっています。なぜ 4 番目の要件が必要となったか論じなさい。

B. 物質的な豊かさと精神的な豊かさとのあいだの二律背反を，ジョンソン大統領はこの演説のなかで，どのような論理と言葉遣いによって調停しているか，論じなさい。

C. 終わりから 2 番目のパラグラフで，ジョンソン大統領はアメリカの歴史について言及しています。これまで読んだ演説のなかでも，アメリカの歴史が頻繁に言及されてきました。このあとのチャプターで取り上げる，カーター，レーガン，クリントン，オバマの演説も何らかのかたちで，アメリカ史に言及しています。ジョンソンがここで語っているアメリカ史を，ケネディのアメリカ史，フランクリン・D・ローズヴェルトのアメリカ史と比較しなさい。またアメリカ合衆国の政治言説のなかで，アメリカの歴史を語ることが，どのような意味や効果を持つか論じなさい。

Chapter 11 | Jimmy Carter's "Crisis of Confidence" Speech (1979)

（Photo by Alarmy）

　1979 年。石油危機により石油価格が倍増し，アメリカ経済は大きな打撃を受ける。ジミー・カーター大統領は，キャンプ・デーヴィッドに側近とともに 10 日間こもり，ありとあらゆる階層のアメリカ人を招いてその声に耳を傾け，国民に向けた演説の構想を練った。

　7 月 15 日，テレビ演説に臨んだカーター大統領は，石油危機以上に，アメリカ国民の「信念の危機（Crisis of Confidence）」について語った。

　演説の暗いしかし真摯なトーンは，アメリカの大統領演説の歴史のなかにあって，きわめて異例なものとなった。

[1] Good Evening:

[2] This a special night for me. Exactly three years ago, on July 15, 1976, I accepted the nomination of my party to run for President of the United States. I promised you a President who is not isolated from the people, who feels your pain, and who shares your dreams, and who draws his strength and his wisdom from you.

[3] During the past three years I've spoken to you on many occasions about national concerns, the energy crisis, reorganizing the government, our nation's economy, and issues of war and especially peace. But over those years the subjects of the speeches, the talks, and the press conferences have become increasingly narrow, focused more and more on what the isolated world of Washington thinks is important. Gradually, you've heard more and more about what the government thinks or what the government should be doing and less and less about our nation's hopes, our dreams, and our vision of the future.

[4] Ten days ago, I had planned to speak to you again about a very important subject — energy. For the fifth time I would have described the urgency of the problem and laid out a series of legislative recommendations to the Congress. But as I was preparing to speak, I began to ask myself the same question that I now know has been troubling many of you: Why have we not

been able to get together as a nation to resolve our serious energy problem?

[5] It's clear that the true problems of our nation are much deeper — deeper than gasoline lines or energy shortages, deeper even than inflation or recession. And I realize more than ever that as President I need your help. So, I decided to reach out and to listen to the voices of America.

[6] I invited to Camp David people from almost every segment of our society — business and labor, teachers and preachers, governors, mayors, and private citizens. And then I left Camp David to listen to other Americans, men and women like you. It has been an extraordinary ten days, and I want to share with you what I've heard.

. . .

[7] These ten days confirmed my belief in the decency and the strength and the wisdom of the American people, but it also bore out some of my longstanding concerns about our nation's underlying problems.

[8] I know, of course, being President, that government actions and legislation can be very important. That's why I've worked hard to put my campaign promises into law, and I have to admit,

with just mixed success. But after listening to the American people, I have been reminded again that all the legislation in the world can't fix what's wrong with America. So, I want to speak to you first tonight about a subject even more serious than energy or inflation. I want to talk to you right now about a fundamental threat to American democracy.

[9] I do not mean our political and civil liberties. They will endure. And I do not refer to the outward strength of America, a nation that is at peace tonight everywhere in the world, with unmatched economic power and military might. The threat is nearly invisible in ordinary ways. It is a crisis of confidence.

[10] It is a crisis that strikes at the very heart and soul and spirit of our national will. We can see this crisis in the growing doubt about the meaning of our own lives and in the loss of a unity of purpose for our nation. The erosion of our confidence in the future is threatening to destroy the social and the political fabric of America.

[11] The confidence that we have always had as a people is not simply some romantic dream or a proverb in a dusty book that we read just on the Fourth of July. It is the idea which founded our nation and has guided our development as a people. Confidence in the future has supported everything else — public institutions and private enterprise, our own families, and the very

Constitution of the United States. Confidence has defined our course and has served as a link between generations. We've always believed in something called progress. We've always had a faith that the days of our children would be better than our own.

[12]　Our people are losing that faith, not only in government itself but in the ability as citizens to serve as the ultimate rulers and shapers of our democracy. As a people we know our past and we are proud of it. Our progress has been part of the living history of America, even the world. We always believed that we were part of a great movement of humanity itself called democracy, involved in the search for freedom; and that belief has always strengthened us in our purpose. But just as we are losing our confidence in the future, we are also beginning to close the door on our past.

[13]　In a nation that was proud of hard work, strong families, close-knit communities, and our faith in God, too many of us now tend to worship self-indulgence and consumption. Human identity is no longer defined by what one does, but by what one owns. But we've discovered that owning things and consuming things does not satisfy our longing for meaning. We've learned that piling up material goods cannot fill the emptiness of lives which have no confidence or purpose.

[14]   The symptoms of this crisis of the American spirit are all around us. For the first time in the history of our country a majority of our people believe that the next five years will be worse than the past five years. Two-thirds of our people do not even vote. The productivity of American workers is actually dropping, and the willingness of Americans to save for the future has fallen below that of all other people in the Western world.

[15]   As you know, there is a growing disrespect for government and for churches and for schools, the news media, and other institutions. This is not a message of happiness or reassurance, but it is the truth and it is a warning.

[16]   These changes did not happen overnight. They've come upon us gradually over the last generation, years that were filled with shocks and tragedy.

[17]   We were sure that ours was a nation of the ballot, not the bullet, until the murders of John Kennedy and Robert Kennedy and Martin Luther King, Jr. We were taught that our armies were always invincible and our causes were always just, only to suffer the agony of Vietnam. We respected the Presidency as a place of honor until the shock of Watergate.

[18]   We remember when the phrase "sound as a dollar" was an expression of absolute dependability, until ten years of inflation

began to shrink our dollar and our savings. We believed that our nation's resources were limitless until 1973 when we had to face a growing dependence on foreign oil. These wounds are still very deep. They have never been healed.

. . .

[19] We often think of conservation only in terms of sacrifice. In fact, it is the most painless and immediate ways of rebuilding our nation's strength. Every gallon of oil each one of us saves is a new form of production. It gives us more freedom, more confidence, that much more control over our own lives.

[20] So, the solution of our energy crisis can also help us to conquer the crisis of the spirit in our country. It can rekindle our sense of unity, our confidence in the future, and give our nation and all of us individually a new sense of purpose.

[21] You know we can do it. We have the natural resources. We have more oil in our shale alone than several Saudi Arabias. We have more coal than any nation on earth. We have the world's highest level of technology. We have the most skilled work force, with innovative genius, and I firmly believe that we have the national will to win this war.

[22] I do not promise you that this struggle for freedom will be

easy. I do not promise a quick way out of our nation's problems, when the truth is that the only way out is an all-out effort. What I do promise you is that I will lead our fight, and I will enforce fairness in our struggle, and I will ensure honesty. And above all, I will act. We can manage the short-term shortages more effectively, and we will; but there are no short-term solutions to our long-range problems. There is simply no way to avoid sacrifice.

[23] Twelve hours from now I will speak again in Kansas City, to expand and to explain further our energy program. Just as the search for solutions to our energy shortages has now led us to a new awareness of our nation's deeper problems, so our willingness to work for those solutions in energy can strengthen us to attack those deeper problems. I will continue to travel this country, to hear the people of America. You can help me to develop a national agenda for the 1980s. I will listen; and I will act. We will act together. These were the promises I made three years ago, and I intend to keep them.

[24] Little by little we can and we must rebuild our confidence. We can spend until we empty our treasuries, and we may summon all the wonders of science. But we can succeed only if we tap our greatest resources — America's people, America's values, and America's confidence. I have seen the strength of America in the inexhaustible resources of our people. In the days

to come, let us renew that strength in the struggle for an energy-secure nation.

[25] In closing, let me say this: I will do my best, but I will not do it alone. Let your voice be heard. Whenever you have a chance, say something good about our country. With God's help and for the sake of our nation, it is time for us to join hands in America. Let us commit ourselves together to a rebirth of the American spirit. Working together with our common faith we cannot fail.

[26] Thank you and good night.

I. この演説の内容について，以下に答えなさい。

  A. この演説のなかで，カーター大統領が答えようとした問いを記したセンテンスを抜き出し，日本語でその意味するところを簡潔に説明しなさい。

  B. 「信念の危機（a crisis of confidence）」という言葉でどのような状況を指しているか。それを定義している<u>パラグラフ</u>を抜き出し，日本語でその意味するところを簡潔に説明しなさい。

  C. カーター大統領は「信念の危機」をもたらしたいくつかの歴史的な出来事に言及しています。どのような出来事か，日本語で簡潔にまとめなさい。

  D. カーター大統領は「信念の危機」を乗り越え，アメリカを再建するためには何が必要だと述べているか。最も重要なメッセージとなっているセンテンスを抜き出し，日本語でその意味するところを簡潔に説明しなさい。

  E. カーター大統領は，演説を結ぶにあたって，国民に何を約束しているか。それを述べている部分（2センテンス）を抜き出し，日本語でその意味するところを簡潔に説明しなさい。

II. 次の一節について，最善の日本語訳を作成してみてください。

In a nation that was proud of hard work, strong families, close-knit communities, and our faith in God, too many of us now tend to worship self-indulgence and consumption. Human identity is no longer defined by what one does, but by what one owns. But we've discovered that owning things and consuming things does not satisfy our longing for meaning. We've learned that piling up material goods cannot fill the emptiness of lives which have no confidence or purpose.

III. 辞書を読み，次の5つの単語がどのような意味をとりうるかを理解しましょう。

concern

I've spoken to you on many occasions about national **concerns**.

It also bore out some of my longstanding **concerns** about our nation' s underlying problems.

erode

The **erosion** of our confidence in the future is threatening to destroy the social and the political fabric of America.

serve as

Confidence has defined our course and has **served as** a link between generations.

agenda

I will continue to travel this country, to hear the people of America. You can help me to develop a national **agenda** for the 1980s.

tap

But we can succeed only if we **tap** our greatest resources ―
America's people, America's values, and America's confidence.

発展的課題

A. カーター大統領のこの演説は，政治演説というよりは，罪の告白
と救済とに関する教会での説教に近いと評されています。それぞ
れどのような部分が，罪の告白と救済とについて語っているか論
じなさい。

B. カーター大統領がキャンプ・デーヴィッドに招いた知識人のなか
で，最も強い影響を大統領に与えたとされるのが，『ナルシシズ
ムの時代（The Culture of Narcissism)』(1979年) の著者，ク
リストファー・ラッシュです。翻訳で同書を読み，ラッシュの思
想がカーター大統領の演説に与えた影響について論じなさい。

C. この演説はアメリカ社会の沈滞感（malaise）について論じた演
説とされています。現代の日本に沈滞感（malaise）があるとす
れば，それはどのような状況か。演説のなかの表現を可能な限り
利用して，150語程度の英語で表現しなさい。

（Photo by Getty Images）

カーター元大統領は，高齢となっても，
低所得者のための家屋建設のボラン
ティア活動の現場に立ち続けた。写真
は 2003 年のもの。

Chapter 12 | Ronald Reagan's "Space Shuttle Challenger Disaster" Speech (1986)

（Photo by Getty Images）

　1986 年 1 月 28 日朝，スペースシャトル「チャレンジャー」が，打ち上げ 73 秒後，全米がテレビ中継を見守るなかで，空中分解し炎上した。乗組員 7 名全員の命が失われた。こうした国家的な惨事が起こった際に，国民の悲しみを癒す追悼演説を行うことは，合衆国大統領の務めである。

　同日夜，レーガン大統領は，予定されていた一般教書演説（The State of the Union Address）を延期し，代わりにホワイトハウスの執務室からテレビ演説を行った。ペギー・ヌーナンが原稿を執筆したこの追悼演説は，アメリカ人の心を深く動かした。

128

(Photo by Getty Images)

[1] Ladies and Gentlemen, I'd planned to speak to you tonight to report on the state of the Union, but the events of earlier today have led me to change those plans. Today is a day for mourning and remembering. Nancy and I are pained to the core by the tragedy of the shuttle Challenger. We know we share this pain with all of the people of our country. This is truly a national loss.

[2] Nineteen years ago, almost to the day, we lost three astronauts in a terrible accident on the ground. But, we've never lost an astronaut in flight; we've never had a tragedy like this. And perhaps we've forgotten the courage it took for the crew of the shuttle; but they, the Challenger Seven, were aware of the dangers, but overcame them and did their jobs brilliantly. We mourn seven heroes: Michael Smith, Dick Scobee, Judith Resnik, Ronald McNair, Ellison Onizuka, Gregory Jarvis, and Christa McAuliffe. We mourn their loss as a nation together.

[3] For the families of the seven, we cannot bear, as you do, the full impact of this tragedy. But we feel the loss, and we're

thinking about you so very much. Your loved ones were daring and brave, and they had that special grace, that special spirit that says, "give me a challenge and I'll meet it with joy." They had a hunger to explore the universe and discover its truths. They wished to serve, and they did. They served all of us.

[4]　We've grown used to wonders in this century. It's hard to dazzle us. But for twenty-five years the United States space program has been doing just that. We've grown used to the idea of space, and perhaps we forget that we've only just begun. We're still pioneers. They, the member of the Challenger crew, were pioneers.

[5]　And I want to say something to the schoolchildren of America who were watching the live coverage of the shuttle's takeoff. I know it is hard to understand, but sometimes painful things like this happen. It's all part of the process of exploration and discovery. It's all part of taking a chance and expanding man's horizons. The future doesn't belong to the fainthearted; it belongs to the brave. The Challenger crew was pulling us into the future, and we'll continue to follow them.

[6]　I've always had great faith in and respect for our space program, and what happened today does nothing to diminish it. We don't hide our space program. We don't keep secrets and cover things up. We do it all up front and in public. That's the

way freedom is, and we wouldn't change it for a minute. We'll continue our quest in space. There will be more shuttle flights and more shuttle crews and, yes, more volunteers, more civilians, more teachers in space. Nothing ends here; our hopes and our journeys continue. I want to add that I wish I could talk to every man and woman who works for NASA or who worked on this mission and tell them: "Your dedication and professionalism have moved and impressed us for decades. And we know of your anguish. We share it."

[7]　There's a coincidence today. On this day 390 years ago, the great explorer Sir Francis Drake died aboard ship off the coast of Panama. In his lifetime the great frontiers were the oceans, and a historian later said, "He lived by the sea, died on it, and was buried in it." Well, today we can say of the challenger crew: Their dedication was, like Drake's, complete.

[8]　The crew of the space shuttle Challenger honored us by the manner in which they lived their lives. We will never forget them, nor the last time we saw them, this morning, as they prepared for the journey and waved goodbye and "slipped the surly bonds of earth" to "touch the face of God."

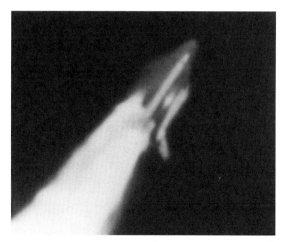

(Photo by Getty Images)

I. この演説の内容について，以下に答えなさい。

    A. 第3パラグラフで，犠牲となった乗組員の家族に向けて，レーガン大統領はメッセージを送っています。メッセージの内容を日本語で簡潔に説明しなさい。

    B. 第5パラグラフで，レーガン大統領は事故をテレビで見ていた子どもたちに向けて，メッセージを送っています。メッセージの内容を日本語で簡潔に説明しなさい。

    C. 第7パラグラフで，レーガン大統領は，チャレンジャーの乗組員と探検家フランシス・ドレイク卿を比較しています。両者のあいだの共通点を言い表したセンテンスを抜き出し，その意味するところをわかりやすく説明しなさい。

II. 次の一節について，最善の日本語訳を作成してみてください。

The crew of the space shuttle Challenger honored us by the manner in which they lived their lives. We will never forget them, nor the last time we saw them, this morning, as they prepared for the journey and waved goodbye and "slipped the surly bonds of earth" to "touch the face of God."

III. 辞書を読み，次の5つの単語がどのような意味をとりうるかを理解しましょう。

loss

This is truly a national **loss**.

But we feel the **loss**, and we're thinking about you so very much.

mourn

We **mourn** seven heroes.

We **mourn** their loss as a nation together.

dare

Your loved ones were **daring** and brave.

belong

The future doesn't **belong** to the fainthearted; it **belongs** to the brave.

dedicate

Their **dedication** was, like Drake's, complete.

発展的課題

A.   この演説は，事故の犠牲者への哀悼の意を綿々と表明するのみ
　　 ならず，この事件に関わる政府の姿勢を表明するものとなって
　　 います。第6パラグラフの冒頭では，この事件によって宇宙開
　　 発プログラムの見直しを行うつもりのないことが表明されてい
　　 ます。それ以外に，どのような政治的表明がなされているか考
　　 えなさい。

B. 演説の末尾は，詩人であり空軍パイロットでもあった John Gillespie Magee Jr. の作品 "High Flight" からの引用となっています。以下に引用する原詩と比較し，下線部の意味がどのようにずらされているか論じなさい。

Oh! I have slipped the surly bonds of earth
And danced the skies on laughter-silvered wings;
Sunward I've climbed, and joined the tumbling mirth
Of sun — split clouds — and done a hundred things

You have not dreamed of — wheeled and soared and swung
High in the sunlit silence. Hov'ring there
I've chased the shouting wind along, and flung
My eager craft through footless halls of air.

Up, up the long delirious, burning blue,
I've topped the windswept heights with easy grace
Where never lark, or even eagle flew —
And, while with silent lifting mind I've trod
The high unsurpassed sanctity of space,
Put out my hand and touched the face of God.

Chapter 13 | Ronald Reagan's Alzheimer's Letter (1994)

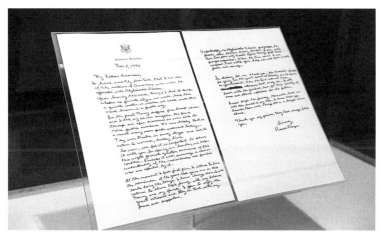

(「レーガン大統領の直筆の手紙」ロナルド・レーガン大統領図書館)

　ロナルド・レーガン（1981年～1989年在任）は，タカ派の対ソ外交を通じ，東西冷戦を終結に導いた大統領である。ハリウッド映画の俳優出身であるレーガン大統領は，国民に語りかけることに巧みな "The Great Communicator" として，現在でもアメリカ国民に親しまれている。

　レーガン大統領は退任後の1994年，国民に向けた手紙を公表し，そのなかで自らがアルツハイマー病の診断を受けたことを明らかにし，そして国民に感動的な別れを告げた。

Nov. 5, 1994

[1] My Fellow Americans,

[2] I have recently been told that I am one of the millions of Americans who will be afflicted with Alzheimer's Disease.

[3] Upon learning this news, Nancy and I had to decide whether as private citizens we would keep this a private matter or whether we would make this news known in a public way.

[4] In the past Nancy suffered from breast cancer and I had my cancer surgeries. We found through our open disclosures we were able to raise public awareness. We were happy that as a result many more people underwent testing.

[5] They were treated in early stages and able to return to normal, healthy lives.

[6] So now, we feel it is important to share it with you. In opening our hearts, we hope this might promote greater awareness of this condition. Perhaps it will encourage a clearer understanding of the individuals and families who are affected by it.

[7] At the moment I feel just fine. I intend to live the remainder

of the years God gives me on this earth doing the things I have always done. I will continue to share life's journey with my beloved Nancy and my family. I plan to enjoy the great outdoors and stay in touch with my friends and supporters.

[8] Unfortunately, as Alzheimer's Disease progresses, the family often bears a heavy burden. I only wish there was some way I could spare Nancy from this painful experience. When the time comes I am confident that with your help she will face it with faith and courage.

[9] In closing let me thank you, the American people for giving me the great honor of allowing me to serve as your President. When the Lord calls me home, whenever that may be, I will leave with the greatest love for this country of ours and eternal optimism for its future.

[10] I now begin the journey that will lead me into the sunset of my life. I know that for America there will always be a bright dawn ahead.

[11] Thank you, my friends. May God always bless you.

Sincerely,
Ronald Reagan

I. この手紙の内容について，以下に答えなさい。

   A. レーガン大統領は，なぜ自らがアルツハイマー病にかかっていることを，アメリカ国民に公表することを選んだのか。その理由を説明した<u>パラグラフ</u>を抜き出し，日本語でその意味するところを簡潔に説明しなさい。

   B. レーガン大統領はこの手紙のなかで，何を最も懸念しているか。それが最もよく表れたセンテンスを抜き出し，日本語でその意味するところを簡潔に説明しなさい。

   C. レーガン大統領はこの手紙のなかで，自らをどのような人間として記憶してほしいと望んでいるか。それが最もよく表れたセンテンスを抜き出し，日本語でその意味するところを簡潔に説明しなさい。

II. 次の一節について，最善の日本語訳を作成してみてください。

In closing let me thank you, the American people for giving me the great honor of allowing me to serve as your President. When the Lord calls me home, whenever that may be, I will leave with the greatest love for this country of ours and eternal optimism for its future.

I now begin the journey that will lead me into the sunset of my life. I know that for America there will always be a bright dawn ahead.

III. 辞書を読み，次の５つの単語がどのような意味をとりうるかを理
　　解しましょう。

afflict

I have recently been told that I am one of the millions of Americans who will be **afflicted** with Alzheimer's Disease.

disclose

In the past Nancy suffered from breast cancer and I had my cancer surgeries. We found through our open **disclosures** we were able to raise public awareness.

share

So now, we feel it is important to **share** it with you.
I will continue to **share** life's journey with my beloved Nancy and my family.
I only wish there was some way I could spare Nancy from this painful experience

spare

I only wish there was some way I could **spare** Nancy from this painful experience.

serve

In closing let me thank you, the American people for giving me the great honor of allowing me to **serve** as your President.

発展的課題

A. 自らのアルツハイマー病という私的な問題に，レーガン元大統領はどのように公的な意味を与えているか，論じなさい。

B. 若い頃，西部劇スターとして知られたレーガン大統領が，西部劇に由来するイメージを，この手紙のなかでどのように活用しているか論じなさい。

C. この手紙の末尾で語られている "optimism" とは何か。この授業で取り上げた他の大統領の言葉も視野に入れながら論じなさい。

D. この手紙の組み立てや表現を可能な限り再利用しながら，故郷へのお別れの手紙，あるいは大学を卒業するにあたってのお別れの手紙を 200 語程度の英語で書いてみましょう。

E. 放送授業のなかでのインタビューにあった表現を可能な限り利用しながら，下の写真の意味を 1 分程度の英語で口頭により説明しなさい。原稿を書いてもよいが，なるべくそれを見ずに話すこと（インタビュー全文テクストは，システム WAKABA で参照できます）。

（撮影：宮本陽一郎）

Chapter 14 | Bill Clinton's Oklahoma Bombing Memorial Prayer Service Address (1995)

(Photo by Diana Walker/Contour by Getty Images)

オクラホマシティ連邦政府ビル爆破事件。

1995年4月19日，オクラホマ州オクラホマシティの連邦政府ビルが，元陸軍兵士ティモシー・マクヴェイらの仕組んだ車爆弾によって爆破される。子ども19人を含む168人が死亡し，680人が負傷した。

事件の4日後の4月23日，犠牲者を追悼する祈祷集会の壇上に，ビル・クリントン大統領が立つ。

[1] Thank you very much, Governor Keating and Mrs. Keating, Reverend Graham, to the families of those who have been lost and wounded, to the people of Oklahoma City, who have endured so much, and the people of this wonderful state, to all of you who are here as our fellow Americans.

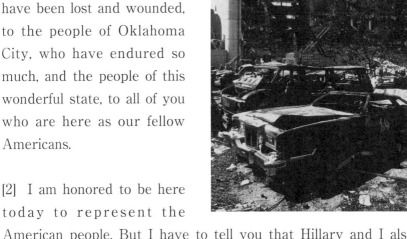

[2] I am honored to be here today to represent the American people. But I have to tell you that Hillary and I also come as parents, as husband and wife, as people who were your neighbors for some of the best years of our lives.

[3] Today our nation joins with you in grief. We mourn with you. We share your hope against hope that some may still survive. We thank all those who have worked so heroically to save lives and to solve this crime — those here in Oklahoma and those who are all across this great land, and many who left their own lives to come here to work hand in hand with you. We pledge to do all we can to help you heal the injured, to rebuild this city, and to bring to justice those who did this evil.

[4] This terrible sin took the lives of our American family, innocent children in that building, only because their parents were trying to be good parents as well as good workers; citizens in the building going about their daily business; and many there who served the rest of us — who worked to help the elderly and the disabled, who worked to support our farmers and our veterans, who worked to enforce our laws and to protect us. Let us say clearly, they served us well, and we are grateful.

[5] But for so many of you they were also neighbors and friends. You saw them at church or the PTA meetings, at the civic clubs, at the ball park. You know them in ways that all the rest of America could not. And to all the members of the families here present who have suffered loss, though we share your grief, your pain is unimaginable, and we know that. We cannot undo it. That is God's work.

[6] Our words seem small beside the loss you have endured. But I found a few I wanted to share today. I've received a lot of letters in these last terrible days. One stood out because it came from a young widow and a mother of three whose own husband was murdered with over 200 other Americans when Pan Am 103 was shot down. Here is what that woman said I should say to you today:

The anger you feel is valid, but you must not allow

yourselves to be consumed by it. The hurt you feel must not be allowed to turn into hate, but instead into the search for justice. The loss you feel must not paralyze your own lives. Instead, you must try to pay tribute to your loved ones by continuing to do all the things they left undone, thus ensuring they did not die in vain.

Wise words from one who also knows.

[7] You have lost too much, but you have not lost everything. And you have certainly not lost America, for we will stand with you for as many tomorrows as it takes.

[8] If ever we needed evidence of that, I could only recall the words of Governor and Mrs. Keating:

If anybody thinks that Americans are mostly mean and selfish, they ought to come to Oklahoma. If anybody thinks Americans have lost the capacity for love and caring and courage, they ought to come to Oklahoma.

To all my fellow Americans beyond this hall, I say, one thing we owe those who have sacrificed is the duty to purge ourselves of the dark forces which gave rise to this evil. They are forces that threaten our common peace, our freedom, our way of life. Let us teach our children that the God of comfort is also the God of righteousness: Those who trouble their own house will inherit the wind. Justice will prevail.

[9] Let us let our own children know that we will stand against the forces of fear. When there is talk of hatred, let us stand up and talk against it. When there is talk of violence, let us stand up and talk against it. In the face of death, let us honor life. As St. Paul admonished us, Let us "not be overcome by evil, but overcome evil with good."

[10] Yesterday, Hillary and I had the privilege of speaking with some children of other federal employees — children like those who were lost here. And one little girl said something we will never forget. She said, "We should all plant a tree in memory of the children." So this morning before we got on the plane to come here, at the White House, we planted that tree in honor of the children of Oklahoma. It was a dogwood with its wonderful spring flower and its deep, enduring roots. It embodies the lesson of the Psalms — that the life of a good person is like a tree whose leaf does not wither.

(Photo by Getty Images)

[11] My fellow Americans, a tree takes a long time to grow, and wounds take a long time to heal. But we must begin. Those who are lost now belong to God. Some day we will be with them. But until that happens, their legacy must be our lives.

[12] Thank you all, and God bless you.

I. この演説の内容について，以下に答えなさい。

 A. クリントン大統領はどのような立場で，この追悼式典に臨みたいと述べているか。それを最も簡潔に言い表したセンテンスを抜き出し，日本語でその意味するところを簡潔に説明しなさい。

 B. この演説のなかに，クリントン大統領は2つの個人的な逸話を盛り込んでいます。それぞれどのようなエピソードか，日本語で簡潔に説明しなさい。

 C. クリントン大統領夫妻は，この日の朝ホワイト・ハウスに植樹したハナミズキにどのような思いをこめたか。それを示したセンテンスを抜き出し，日本語でその意味するところを簡潔に説明しなさい。

 D. この演説のなかで，クリントン大統領は国民に何を訴えかけているか。最も重要なメッセージとなっているセンテンスを抜き出し，日本語でその意味するところを簡潔に説明しなさい。

II. 次の一節について，最善の日本語訳を作成してみてください。

To all my fellow Americans beyond this hall, I say, one thing we owe those who have sacrificed is the duty to purge ourselves of the dark forces which gave rise to this evil. They are forces that threaten our common peace, our freedom, our way of life. Let us teach our children that the God of comfort is also the God of righteousness: Those who trouble their own house will inherit the wind. Justice will prevail.

III. 辞書を読み，次の 5 つの単語がどのような意味をとりうるかを理
　　解しましょう。

endure

The people of Oklahoma City, who have **endured** so much.

Our words seem small beside the loss you have **endured**.

It was a dogwood with its wonderful spring flower and its deep,
enduring roots.

consume

The anger you feel is valid, but you must not allow yourselves to be
consumed by it.

tribute

You must try to pay **tribute** to your loved ones by continuing to do
all the things they left undone, thus ensuring they did not die in
vain.

admonish

As St. Paul **admonished** us, Let us "not be overcome by evil, but
overcome evil with good."

legacy

Their **legacy** must be our lives.

発展的課題

A. この追悼演説のなかで，クリントン大統領は「テロリズム」や「爆弾」を直接指し示す言葉を一切使っていません。それはなぜでしょうか。

B. この演説のなかで，クリントン大統領は自分と聴衆とのあいだの距離を近づけるために，どのような工夫をしていますか。

C. クリントン大統領はテロリズムの脅威に対して，どのような姿勢で臨もうとしているか，この追悼演説から読み取れることを論じなさい。

D. 放送授業のなかでのカリ・ワトキンズ館長へのインタビューにあった表現を可能な限り利用しながら，日本にある記念碑（例えば沖縄の平和の塔）の意味を，150 語程度の英語で書きなさい（インタビュー全文テクストは，システム WAKABA で参照できます）。

E. 放送授業のなかでのカリ・ワトキンズ館長へのインタビューにあった表現を可能な限り利用しながら，次頁の写真の意味を，1 分程度の英語で口頭により説明しなさい。原稿を書いてもかまいませんが，なるべくそれを見ずに話すこと（インタビュー全文テクストは，システム WAKABA で参照できます）。

150

(Photo by Getty Images)

Chapter 15 | Barack Obama's "A More Perfect Union" Speech (2008)

(Photo by Getty Images)

　2008年の大統領選挙に立候補したバラク・オバマは，1つの文化現象といってよいほどの強い支持を集めた。

　しかし，民主党の予備選挙を前にした2008年3月，オバマ候補がかつて私淑していたアフリカ系アメリカ人牧師ジェレマイア・ライトの反アメリカ的な説教のビデオ——とりわけ「神よアメリカを断罪せよ（God damn America）という一節——が，マスコミに流れ，オバマ候補は窮地に立たされる。

　アメリカの世論は二分され，人種をめぐり大きな亀裂を見せる。

　3月8日，オバマ候補はアメリカ合衆国憲法が起草されたフィラデルフィアを訪れ，その前文にある「より完璧な連邦（a more perfect union）」という言葉をタイトルとする，彼の最も雄弁な演説を行う。

[1] The profound mistake of Reverend Wright's sermons is not that he spoke about racism in our society. It's that he spoke as if our society was static; as if no progress had been made; as if this country — a country that has made it possible for one of his own members to run for the highest office in the land and build a coalition of white and black, Latino and Asian, rich and poor, young and old — is still irrevocably bound to a tragic past. But what we know — what we have seen — is that America can change. That is the true genius of this nation. What we have already achieved gives us hope — the audacity to hope — for what we can and must achieve tomorrow.

[2] In the white community, the path to a more perfect union means acknowledging that what ails the African-American community does not just exist in the minds of black people; that the legacy of discrimination — and current incidents of discrimination, while less overt than in the past — are real and must be addressed, not just with words, but with deeds, by investing in our schools and our communities; by enforcing our civil rights laws and ensuring fairness in our criminal justice system; by providing this generation with ladders of opportunity that were unavailable for previous generations. It requires all Americans to realize that your dreams do not have to come at the expense of my dreams; that investing in the health, welfare and education of black and brown and white children will ultimately help all of America prosper.

[3] In the end, then, what is called for is nothing more and nothing less than what all the world's great religions demand — that we do unto others as we would have them do unto us. Let us be our brother's keeper, scripture tells us. Let us be our sister's keeper. Let us find that common stake we all have in one another, and let our politics reflect that spirit as well.

[4] For we have a choice in this country. We can accept a politics that breeds division and conflict and cynicism. We can tackle race only as spectacle — as we did in the O.J. trial — or in the wake of tragedy — as we did in the aftermath of Katrina — or as fodder for the nightly news. We can play Reverend Wright's sermons on every channel, every day and talk about them from now until the election, and make the only question in this campaign whether or not the American people think that I somehow believe or sympathize with his most offensive words. We can pounce on some gaffe by a Hillary supporter as evidence that she's playing the race card, or we can speculate on whether white men will all flock to John McCain in the general election regardless of his policies.

[5] We can do that.

[6] But if we do, I can tell you that in the next election, we'll be talking about some other distraction. And then another one. And then another one. And nothing will change.

[7] That is one option. Or, at this moment, in this election, we can come together and say, "Not this time." This time, we want to talk about the crumbling schools that are stealing the future of black children and white children and Asian children and Hispanic children and Native American children. This time, we want to reject the cynicism that tells us that these kids can't learn; that those kids who don't look like us are somebody else's problem. The children of America are not those kids, they are our kids, and we will not let them fall behind in a 21st century economy. Not this time.

[8] This time we want to talk about how the lines in the emergency room are filled with whites and blacks and Hispanics who do not have health care, who don't have the power on their own to overcome the special interests in Washington, but who can take them on if we do it together.

[9] This time, we want to talk about the shuttered mills that once provided a decent life for men and women of every race, and the homes for sale that once belonged to Americans from every religion, every region, every walk of life. This time, we want to talk about the fact that the real problem is not that someone who doesn't look like you might take your job; it's that the corporation you work for will ship it overseas for nothing more than a profit.

[10] This time, we want to talk about the men and women of every color and creed who serve together and fight together and bleed together under the same proud flag. We want to talk about how to bring them home from a war that should have never been authorized and should have never been waged. And we want to talk about how we'll show our patriotism by caring for them and their families, and giving them the benefits that they have earned.

[11] I would not be running for President if I didn't believe with all my heart that this is what the vast majority of Americans want for this country. This union may never be perfect, but generation after generation has shown that it can always be perfected. And today, whenever I find myself feeling doubtful or cynical about this possibility, what gives me the most hope is the next generation — the young people whose attitudes and beliefs and openness to change have already made history in this election.

[12] There is one story in particularly that I'd like to leave you with today — a story I told when I had the great honor of speaking on Dr. King's birthday at his home church, Ebenezer Baptist, in Atlanta.

[13] There is a young, 23-year-old white woman named Ashley Baia who organized for our campaign in Florence, S.C. She had

been working to organize a mostly African-American community since the beginning of this campaign, and one day she was at a roundtable discussion where everyone went around telling their story and why they were there.

[14] And Ashley said that when she was 9 years old, her mother got cancer. And because she had to miss days of work, she was let go and lost her health care. They had to file for bankruptcy, and that's when Ashley decided that she had to do something to help her mom.

[15] She knew that food was one of their most expensive costs, and so Ashley convinced her mother that what she really liked and really wanted to eat more than anything else was mustard and relish sandwiches — because that was the cheapest way to eat. That's the mind of a 9-year-old.

[16] She did this for a year until her mom got better. So she told everyone at the roundtable that the reason she joined our campaign was so that she could help the millions of other children in the country who want and need to help their parents, too.

[17] Now, Ashley might have made a different choice. Perhaps somebody told her along the way that the source of her mother's

problems were blacks who were on welfare and too lazy to work, or Hispanics who were coming into the country illegally. But she didn't. She sought out allies in her fight against injustice.

[18] Anyway, Ashley finishes her story and then goes around the room and asks everyone else why they're supporting the campaign. They all have different stories and different reasons. Many bring up a specific issue. And finally they come to this elderly black man who's been sitting there quietly the entire time. And Ashley asks him why he's there. And he does not bring up a specific issue. He does not say health care or the economy. He does not say education or the war. He does not say that he was there because of Barack Obama. He simply says to everyone in the room, "I am here because of Ashley."

[19] "I'm here because of Ashley." By itself, that single moment of recognition between that young white girl and that old black man is not enough. It is not enough to give health care to the sick, or jobs to the jobless, or education to our children.

[20] But it is where we start. It is where our union grows stronger. And as so many generations have come to realize over the course of the 221 years since a band of patriots signed that document right here in Philadelphia, that is where the perfection begins.

I. この演説の内容について，以下に答えなさい。

  A. 第1パラグラフで，オバマ候補はライト牧師の考え方を，"static"
  であると批判しています。ここでの"static"とはどのような意味
  か，日本語で簡潔に説明しなさい。

  B. 第4パラグラフでいくつかの事件が列挙されていますが，これら
  は何の例示として挙げられているのでしょうか。本文中から最も
  適切な単語1語を抜き出し，その意味するところを日本語で分か
  りやすく説明しなさい。

  C. 第7〜10パラグラフで，オバマ候補は今ほんとうにアメリカが
  取り組むべき問題を列挙しています。そのなかから理解できたも
  の3つを選び，簡潔に意味するところを日本語で説明しなさい。

  D. オバマ候補は，アシュレー・バイアという女性に関する逸話で締
  めくくっています。この逸話はどのようなメッセージを伝えよう
  とするものか，日本語で簡潔に説明しなさい。

II. 次の一節について，最善の日本語訳を作成してみてください。

I would not be running for President if I didn't believe with all
my heart that this is what the vast majority of Americans want
for this country. This union may never be perfect, but generation
after generation has shown that it can always be perfected. And
today, whenever I find myself feeling doubtful or cynical about
this possibility, what gives me the most hope is the next
generation — the young people whose attitudes and beliefs and

openness to change have already made history in this election.

III. 辞書を読み，次の5つの単語がどのような意味をとりうるかを理
解しましょう。

irrevocable
This country is still **irrevocably** bound to a tragic past.

acknowledge
In the white community, the path to a more perfect union means
acknowledging that what ails the African-American community
does not just exist in the minds of black people

addressed
The legacy of discrimination are real and must be **addressed**.

at the **expense** of
Your dreams do not have to come at the **expense** of my dreams.

recognition
By itself, that single moment of **recognition** between that young
white girl and that old black man is not enough.

A. オバマ候補は，その選挙キャンペーンのスローガンであった "Yes we can" "Hope and Change" "Audacity to Hope" を，この演説の なかにどのように盛り込んでいるか，指摘しなさい。

B. この演説のなかで，反復が効果的に用いられている箇所を指摘し なさい。

C. この演説を，直接的に自らの信条を述べた文──例えば第 11 パ ラグラフ──ではなく，アシュレー・バイアという女性に関する 逸話で締めくくることは，どのような効果を持っているか，論じ なさい。

（Photo by Getty Images）

162

問　題　解　答

Chapter 2

問1

I. Thesis: Cats make excellent housepets.

II. Topic: people enjoy the companionship of cats.

    A. Cats are affectionate.

    B. Cats are playful.

    C. Cats can be trained.

III. Topic: Cats are civilized.

    D. Cats do not bark.

    E. Cats don't have accidents.

    F. Cats do have claws. But provisions can be made.

IV. Topic: Ease of care.

    G. Cats do not have to be walked.

    H. Cats also take care of their own grooming.

    I. Cats can be left home alone.

V. Conclusion: Cats are the ideal housepet.

問2

1.　ネコはよいペットだ。

2.1　ネコは吠えない。

  2　ネコは粗相をしない。

  3　ネコには爪があるが，対策可能。

3.1　散歩をさせなくてよい。

  2　自分で毛づくろいをする。

  3　家にひとりで置いておいても大丈夫。

4.　居住空間が狭い人や，時間がない人。

Chapter 3

I. A. 私は，過酷で闘争的な人生を生きようという私の信条を，みなさんにお話したい。安逸な生活というものは，国家にとっても一人の人間にとっても，ためにならないものである。平和を求める臆病さではなく，努力して何かを勝ち取ることこそがすばらしい。肉体労働をしなくてもすむような豊かな境遇にある人は，だからといって享楽に走ってはいけない。健全な国家は，健全な生き方をしている男女によって支えられるのである。アメリカ合衆国は，その意味で輝かしい歴史を持っている。私たちアメリカ人は，その信ずるところが正しい限りにおいて。肉体的・精神的な闘いを恐れてはならない。

   B. 安逸を求めず，からだを酷使し，危険に自ら挑戦し，高い理想のために闘う生き方。

   C. And if we had thus avoided it, we would have shown that we were weaklings, and that we were unfit to stand among the great nations of the earth.
   もし南北戦争を避けて平和を求めていたら，アメリカは弱い国になってしまい，地上の偉大な国家に伍することができなかっただろう。

II. もし私たちが戦争を避けてしまっていたら，それは私たちが脆弱な国であるということを示すことになっていたでしょう。この地上の偉大な国々に伍することはできなかったでしょう。私たちの祖先の血のなかに鉄の意志が通っていたことを，神に感謝するべきです。祖先たちはリンカーンの叡智を支持し，剣や銃をとってグラント将軍の軍隊に加わったのです！歴史の強大な力に立ち向かった男たち，偉大な南北戦争を勝利に導いた男たち——その子孫である私たちは，祖先の信じた神に感謝しましょう。平和を求めなさいという臆病な知恵を退けたことを。苦しみと別れ，限りない悲しみと絶望に，怯むことなく立ち向かったことを。そして何年にもわたる闘いを勝ち抜いたのです。そのおかげで，奴隷は解放され，南北に分断された連邦が再び統合され，アメリカという偉大な国家は再び鎧を身につけ

た女王のように君臨したのです。

Chapter 4

I. A. In every dark hour of our national life a leadership of frankness and vigor has met with that understanding and support of the people themselves which is essential to victory.

国民に対し誠実で，たくましい精神。

B. I am convinced that you will again give that support to leadership in these critical days.

危機に瀕して指導者を支持する精神。

C. Practices of the unscrupulous money changers stand indicted in the court of public opinion, rejected by the hearts and minds of men.

非良心的な銀行家たちを国民は許さない。

D. The measure of the restoration lies in the extent to which we apply social values more noble than mere monetary profit.

金銭的な富より大切なのは，社会的な価値である。大恐慌からの復興はそれにかかっている。

II. それゆえに，私はこのように確信します。いま恐れるべきは，恐れのみです。恐れ——つまり正体不明の，愚かで理不尽な恐れ。それが立ち直り前に進もうとする努力を麻痺させている。この国の歴史のなかの暗い瞬間には，必ず誠実で力強い指導者が現れ，そしてそのような指導者が国民の理解と支持を受けてきました。それこそが勝利のために不可欠なのです。

Chapter 5

I. A. A comparatively small part of the money that you put into the bank is kept in currency — an amount which in normal times is wholly sufficient to cover the cash needs of the average citizen.

預金者が銀行に預けたお金のうち，通貨として銀行に置かれるのは，そのごく一部に過ぎない。

B. 第3パラグラフ。不安に駆られた多くの人々が，一斉に預金の払い戻しを求め，銀行が対応できなくなった。もし対応しようとすれば，銀行は実際の価値よりもはるかに低い値段で資産を売却しなければならなかった。

C. After all, there is an element in the readjustment of our financial system more important than currency, more important than gold, and that is the confidence of the people themselves.
アメリカの金融システムを立て直すために，お金より大切なのは信頼である。

II. 別に預言者でなくても誰でも分かることですが，人々が自分のお金を取り戻せると分かれば，つまりまっとうな使い道のためのお金は取り戻せると分かれば，恐れという亡霊は消えて無くなるんです。人々は，お金を安全に預かってくれて，しかも必要なときにはいつでも使えるという場所に，お金を預けるでしょう。だから，みなさん，お金をベッドのマットレスの下に隠したりするよりは，再開した銀行に預けたほうが，ずっと安心ですよ。私が保証します。

Chapter 6

I. A. The object is to make people everywhere conscious of the importance of human rights and freedoms.
世界中の人々に，人権と自由の大切さを意識してもらうこと。

B. The reason for that is that these are spoken of and emphasized in the Charter of the United Nations, and the declaration was written to elaborate the rights already mentioned in the charter and to emphasize also, for all of us, the fact that the building of human rights would be one of the foundation stones, on which we would build in the world, an atmosphere in which peace can grow.

世界人権宣言は，すでに国連憲章のなかに書かれている自由と人権の理念を，さらに具体化し，そして平和な世界の礎として位置づけるものである。

C. If we observe these rights, for ourselves and for others, I think we will find that it is easier in the world to build peace because war destroys all human rights and freedoms, so in fighting for those we fight for peace.

戦争とは，人権と自由の破壊にほかならず，また私たちがお互いの人権を大切にすれば，平和な世界は作りやすくなる。

II. 私たちは，同じ人間である仲間たちが人権と自由を持つことを望んでしかるべきでしょう。人権と自由があればこそ，みんなが尊厳を持ち，自分が人間であることを実感し，そして堂々とこの地上を歩き，お互いの顔をまっすぐに見つめることができるのです。

Chapter 7

I. A. 自由主義と全体主義

B. 第6パラグラフ。ギリシャが共産主義の手に落ちれば，それは隣国であるトルコに直ちに影響を及ぼし，さらに中東諸国に混乱（つまり共産主義）が広がる。さらに第二次世界大戦の戦禍の残るヨーロッパの国々にも，深刻な影響を及ぼすだろう。

C. 第11パラグラフ。The seeds of totalitarian regimes are nurtured by misery and want.

全体主義は，貧困と欠乏によって育てられるものである。

D. The free peoples of the world look to us for support in maintaining their freedoms.

全世界の自由を享受している人々は，その自由を維持するため，アメリ

カに頼っている。

II. 私が提案しているギリシャとトルコに対する支援は，アメリカ合衆国が第
二次世界大戦に投じた予算の 0.1 パーセントにすぎません。この投資を守
り，この投資が無意味にならないように保障していくということは，まっ
たく常識にかなったことです。全体主義の政治という種は，貧困と欠乏に
よって育まれます。それは，貧しさと戦乱という悪の土壌のもとで，はび
こり育っていきます。そして人々がよりよい生活への希望を失ったとき，
蔓延するのです。

Chapter 8

I. A. And having now confirmed and completed our evaluation of the
evidence and our decision on a course of action, this Government
feels obliged to report this new crisis to you in fullest detail.
いま起こっている危機的状況とそれに対する政府の対応について，その
詳細を国民に報告する。

B. Each of these missiles, in short, is capable of striking Washington,
D.C., the Panama Canal, Cape Canaveral, Mexico City, or any
other city in the southeastern part of the United States, in
Central America, or in the Caribbean area.
キューバに配備されるミサイルは，ワシントン DC さらにはメキシコ・
シティーやパナマ運河までも，核攻撃可能な範囲としている。

C. 第 9 ～ 11 パラグラフ。
These new weapons are not in your interest.
ソビエトのミサイルを配備することは，キューバ国民自身のためになら
ない。

D. Our goal is not the victory of might, but the vindication of
right — not peace at the expense of freedom, but both peace and
freedom, here in this hemisphere, and, we hope, around the

168

world.

アメリカの目的はソビエトに勝つことではなく，世界の正義と平和と自由を守ることだ。

II. 私たちが選んだ道は，危険に満ちた道です。どのような道であれ，危険はつきものです。しかしこの道は，私たちアメリカ人の，国民としての尊厳と勇気，のみならず私たちが世界のなかで果たそうとする役割に，最もふさわしいものです。自由を得るための代償は常に高い──そしてアメリカ人は，いつもそういう高い代償を支払ってきました。それに対して，私たちアメリカ人が絶対に選ばない道──それは他国に対して降伏し服従するという道です。

私たちが目指すのは，力により勝利することではありません。そうではなく，私たちが正しいということを証明することです。自由を捨ててまで手に入れる平和ではなく，平和と自由の両方を守るのです。西半球における自由と平和，そして願わくは［共産圏も含む］全世界の平和を。

ご静聴ありがとうございました。それではおやすみなさい。

Chapter 9

I. A. I have, therefore, chosen this time and this place to discuss a topic on which ignorance too often abounds and the truth is too rarely perceived — yet it is the most important topic on earth: world peace.

世界平和というのは，しばしば無知のなかで語られ，めったにその真実が認識されない。

B. 〔5〕 I speak of peace because of the new face of war. Total war <u>makes no sense</u> in an age when great powers can maintain large and relatively invulnerable nuclear forces and refuse to surrender without resort to those forces. It <u>makes no sense</u> in an age when a single nuclear weapon contains almost ten times the explosive force delivered by all the allied air forces in the Second World War. It <u>makes no sense</u> in an age when the deadly poisons produced by a nuclear exchange would be carried by wind and water and soil and seed to the far corners of the globe and to generations yet unborn. 繰り返される表現："makes no sense"

C.

absolute peace	concept	good will	sudden revolution	static
practical peace	process	concrete actions	gradual evolution	dynamic

II. どのような平和について，私は語るのでしょう？どのような平和を私たちは求めるのでしょう？アメリカの軍事力によって押しつけられる，アメリカ中心の平和ではありません。墓場の平和や奴隷に与えられる平和でもありません。そうではなく本物の平和──この地球の上で私たちが享受する生を，生きるに値するものにしてくれるような平和，人々が諸国が成長し希望を持ち，そして子孫のためによりよい世界を残すことができるような，そういう平和。アメリカ人だけのための平和ではなく，すべての人のための平和。私たちの時代のさしあたりの平和ではなく，時代を超えるような平和です。

Chapter 10

I. A. ①貧困や人種差別のない，豊かで自由な社会。②すべての人に教育の機会が与えられた，教養豊かな社会。③自然との絆を新たにすることのできる社会。④新たな目標に向かって挑戦し続ける社会。

B. ①宗教や人種による差別をなくすための闘い。②貧困をなくすための闘い。③恒久的な平和を実現するための闘い。④物質的な豊かさよりも大切なものがあることを証明する＜偉大な社会＞を築くための闘い。

C. The challenge of the next half century is whether we have the wisdom to use that wealth to enrich and elevate our national life, and to advance the quality of our American civilization.

物質的な富は，精神的な豊かさを実現するための手段である。それを実現できるかどうかは，私たちの知力にかかっている。

II. みなさんも＜偉大な社会＞を作るための闘いに参加しようではありませんか。そしてアメリカ社会の物質的な豊かさは，心と精神のためのより豊かな生活を築く礎に過ぎないことを証明しましょう。それは勝ち目のない闘いだと言う臆病な者もいるでしょう。富には魂はないと絶望する者もいるでしょう。私はそうは思いません。私たちには私たちが求めるような文明を築く力があるんです。しかしそのような社会を築くためには，国民のみなさんの意志と努力と勇気が必要なのです。

Chapter 11

I. A. But as I was preparing to speak, I began to ask myself the same question that I now know has been troubling many of you: Why have we not been able to get together as a nation to resolve our serious energy problem?

なぜエネルギー危機を乗り切るために国民が団結できないのか。

B. It is a crisis that strikes at the very heart and soul and spirit of our national will. We can see this crisis in the growing doubt about the meaning of our own lives and in the loss of a unity of purpose for our nation. The erosion of our confidence in the future is threatening to destroy the social and the political fabric of America.

アメリカ人として生きることの意味に対する懐疑が生まれ，国家としての団結が失われた。

C. ジョン・F・ケネディ，ロバート・ケネディ，マーティン・ルーサー・キング・ジュニアの暗殺。ヴェトナム戦争。ウォーターゲート事件。

D. But we can succeed only if we tap our greatest resources —

America's people, America's values, and America's confidence.
アメリカの本来の国民性，価値観，信念に立ち返ること。

E. What I do promise you is that I will lead our fight, and I will enforce fairness in our struggle, and I will ensure honesty. And above all, I will act.
いま国家が直面している問題を克服するため，国民の先頭に立ち，そのなかでの公正さを保ち，正直に語ること，そしてなによりも行動すること。

II. アメリカ人は，勤勉であること，家族の強い絆を持つこと，そして敬虔な信仰を持つことを誇りとしてきました。にもかかわらず，あまりにも多くのアメリカ人が，安逸さと消費に身をやつしてきました。人間の本質が，何をするかではなく，何を所有しているかによって語られるようになってしまった。しかし私たちは，物を所有したり消費したりすることが，生きがいを与えてくれるものではないということを知っています。財を築いたところで，それは信念も目的もない人生の虚しさを埋め合わせてくれるものではありません。

Chapter 12

I. A. あなた方のご家族は，自ら進んで困難にチャレンジする勇気をもった人々であり，国民のために命を捧げた。

B. 探検や発明には，時としてこのような痛ましい犠牲が伴うことを理解してほしい。

C. Well, today we can say of the challenger crew: Their dedication was, like Drake's, complete.
自分が探検しようとする世界に身を捧げ尽くした。

II. スペースシャトル「チャレンジャー」の乗組員たちは，その生き様を通じて，私たちアメリカ人に誇りをもたらしてくれました。私たちは彼らを忘れません。最後に私たちが彼らを見たときの姿を。今朝，彼らは旅支度をして

私たちに手を振って別れを告げ，そして「地球の無愛想な重力の外に滑り出て」「神の顔に手を触れた」のです。

Chapter 13

I. A. So now, we feel it is important to share it with you. In opening our hearts, we hope this might promote greater awareness of this condition. Perhaps it will encourage a clearer understanding of the individuals and families who are affected by it.

アルツハイマー病に対する国民の意識を高め，患者とその家族に対する理解を深めるため。

B. Unfortunately, as Alzheimer's Disease progresses, the family often bears a heavy burden.

今後，病状が進行していった場合の，家族（妻ナンシー）の負担。

C. When the Lord calls me home, whenever that may be, I will leave with the greatest love for this country of ours and eternal optimism for its future.

国を愛し，その明るい未来を信じ続けた人間として記憶してほしい。

II. 最後に，私に大統領として奉仕する機会を与えてくれた国民のみなさんに，お礼を申し上げたい。私が主のもとに召されるのがいつのことになるか分かりませんが，私はこの国をこよなく愛し，その明るい未来を信じ続けた人間として旅立つことになるでしょう。私はこれから人生の夕暮れに向けて旅立ちます。そしてアメリカの行く手には，常に眩いばかりの夜明けが待っていると信じています。

Chapter 14

I. A. But I have to tell you that Hillary and I also come as parents, as husband and wife, as people who were your neighbors for some of the best years of our lives.

大統領としてではなく，家族・隣人の一人としてこの追悼祈祷式に臨みたい。

B. ・事件以来，国民から寄せられたたくさんの手紙のなかのひとつに書いてあったこと。

・その日の朝，ホワイト・ハウスでヒラリーとともに植樹をしたこと。

C. It was a dogwood with its wonderful spring flower and its deep, enduring roots. It embodies the lesson of the Psalms — that the life of a good person is like a tree whose leaf does not wither.
善良な人間の行いは，樹のようなものであり，決して枯れることがない。

D. But we must begin.
今回の事件の心の傷を癒すには時間がかかるが，しかし私たちはそれをいますぐに始めなければならない。

II. この会場の外にいる，アメリカ国民のみなさんにも申し上げたい。今回の事件の犠牲となった人々のためにも，私たちは私たちの心のなかから暗い感情を洗い流さなければならない。そもそも今回の事件を生んだのは，そういう暗い感情なのです。そういう感情の持つ力が，私たちみんなの平和と自由とアメリカ的な生き方を脅かすのです。私たちの子孫に教えましょう。私たちを癒す神は，正義を守る神でもあります。私たちの平穏を脅かした人間は，必ずその報いを受けます。正義は必ず勝利するのです。

Chapter 15

I. A. アメリカが絶えず変化するダイナミックな国であるということに目を閉ざし，その過去に縛られている。

B. distraction. より重要な問題から国民の関心をそらせてしまうような，つまらない問題。

C. 次の中からいずれか3つ。1.教育問題，2.医療問題，3.企業と雇用の海外流出，4.イラク戦争の早期終結，5.帰還兵士とその家族への生活保障。

D. 人種の違いを超えた共通の問題がある。お互いの抱える共通の問題に

ついて，人種の違いを超えて共感し合うことが，「より完璧な連邦」に向けての出発点である。

II. 私が大統領選挙に出馬したのは，これこそが大多数のアメリカ人が求めていることだと，心の底から信じるからこそです。この連邦，さまざまな人々のこの団結は，けっして完璧なものにはならないのかもしれません。しかし何世代にもわたるアメリカ人が，完璧なものとなる可能性がすぐそこにあるということを示し続けてきたのです。そして現在，理想の実現が不可能に思えたり，ばかばかしく思えてきたりするとき，私に希望を与えてくれるのは，次の世代の人々です。若い人々の，生き方，信念，そして変革に対して前向きな姿勢──それは今回の大統領選挙で，もうすでに歴史的な出来事になったのではありませんか。

著者紹介

宮本 陽一郎 (みやもと・よういちろう)

1955 年　　　東京都に生まれる
1981 年　　　東京大学大学院人文科学研究科課程終始課程修了
1981-83 年　　東京大学助手
1983-94 年　　成蹊大学講師・助教授
1994-2017 年　筑波大学准教授・教授
2018 年～　　放送大学教授
現在　　　放送大学教授・筑波大学名誉教授
専攻　　　アメリカ文学, カルチュラル・スタディーズ
主な著書・訳書
　　　『モダンの黄昏―帝国主義の改体とポストモダンの生成』
　　　研究社, 2002 年
　　　『アトミック・メロドラマ―冷戦アメリカのドラマトゥル
　　　ギー』彩流社, 2016 年
　　　『知の版図―英米文学と知識の枠組み』(共編著) 悠書館,
　　　2008 年
　　　Hemingway, Cuba, and the Cuban Works. (分担著) Kent
　　　State University Press, 2014.
　　　ジョン・ガードナー著『オクトーバー・ライト』集英社,
　　　1981 年
　　　チャールズ・ジョンソン著『中間航路』早川書房, 1995 年

放送大学教材　1420119-1-2011（テレビ）

英語で読む大統領演説

発　行　　2020 年 3 月 20 日　第 1 刷

著　者　　宮本陽一郎

発行所　　一般財団法人　放送大学教育振興会
　　　　　〒105-0001　東京都港区虎ノ門 1-14-1　郵政福祉琴平ビル
　　　　　電話　03（3502）2750

Printed in Japan　ISBN978-4-595-32223-5　C1382